CO-OPERATIVES : ITS GROWTH AND NEW DIMENSIONS

Co-operatives : Its Growth and New Dimensions

Edited by :
Dr. S. N. Tripathy

DISCOVERY PUBLISHING HOUSE
NEW DELHI – 110 002

First Published-2000
Reprinted-2010
ISBN 81-7141-521-0

DISCOVERY PUBLISHING HOUSE
4831/24, Ansari Road, Prahlad Street,
Darya Ganj, New Delhi-110002 (India)
Phone: 3279245 · Fax: 91-11-3253475
E-mail:dph@indiatimes.com

Laser Typeset by:
Allied Computers,
Karnal (Haryana)

Printed at:
Mehra Offset Press
Delhi

Preface

The Co-operative movement was introduced in India in the early years of this century with the Primary objective of relieving the peasants from the burden of indebtedness and excessively high rate of interest through the supply of credit at a lower rate of interest.

Thus, co-operatives serve as alternative sources to villagers who otherwise depend on money-lenders. Co-operatives today cover the entire spectrum of activities in rural areas. The co-operative movement is responsible for a comprehensive development of primary agricultural credit societies to function as multi-purpose, viable units.

Thus, essentially, the co-operative movement in our country though began as a credit movement, ultimately non-credit activities were introduced in the co-operative structure. However, the credit activities still continued to constitute the most significant element of the co-operative movement.

In our country, in view of the under-employment of resources and extremely unfavourable land-man ratio, co-operative farming is the only possible way to meet the demand for increased agricultural production. If the farming socieities can not indicate profit, farmers will not be interested to participate in the movement.

Successful implementation of land reform measures, mainly a programme for consolidation of land holdings, should be linked with the co-operative farming. In areas of extremely uneconomic holdings, the best method to achieve consolidation is through the establishment of co-operative farming activities. The Government should ensure the co-operation and village and cottage industries. Co-operatives are destined to emerge as dominant undertakings in vital sectors of the economy like agriculture, fisheries, housing distribution of consumer goods; industrial development, handloom sector etc.

"Co-operatives : Growth and New Dimensions"—contain 15 contributions of eminent authors of different disciplines. This volume examines the entire gamut of issues relating to co-operative sector, and its role in developing the Indian economy, covering development problems and prospects.

Prof. Sain's paper, "Role of Industrial Co-operatives in the context of New Industrial Policy and for Rural and Urban Development" Portrays the role of industrial co-operatives in the planned economic development of our economy. The valuable role played by industrial co-operatives in the rural upliftment has been briefly highlighted in this unique paper. The weakness of industrial co-operatives have been outlined and suggestions for strengthening the co-operatives have been forwarded.

The role of agricultural credit being indispensable for the development of agricultural sector and the economy as a whole, a few papers highlight the importance, trend and role of agricultural co-operative credit.

Prof. S. P. Gupta's paper deals with "Credit and Its Use in Technological Development of Agriculture." The study covers the data collected from the Raipur district of Madhya Pradesh. The socio-economic profile of the sample farmers have been presented in this paper. The utilisation pattern of co-operative credit and the impact of co-operative credit in the level of output and income has been estimated.

Dr. S. Lakshman's paper, "Farm Credit and Non-farm Credit Recovery Performance of Kartallipulayam Primary Agricultural Co-operative Bank in Erode district" examines the trend of growth of membership, share capital, investment details, deposit position, recovery of loans etc.

In their joint authorship the study by Prof. J.P. Mishra and Shri Kumar Rawat in the Hamirpur district of Uttar Pradesh evaluates the role of co-operative credit in the development of agricultural sector. Making a historial review of growth of agricultural credit, the study highlights the progress, and role of agricultural co-operatives and the impact of credit on agricultural development. Through tabular analysis of data, the study throws light on progress of PACs in Uttar Pradesh, credit needs and their availability, productivity of crops, crop intensity, sources of loans purpose-wise loans, cost of loans, the gap between needs and availability of co-operative loans, repayment position and level of investment, employment and income etc.

In their joint paper Dr. Patra, Dr. (Mrs.) Das and Miss Nayak have presented plan-wise performance of co-operative credit institutions in Orissa in the Developmental frame-work of the economy, statistical tools like multiple regression model etc. have been adopted alongwith future strategies of the co-operative sector.

Smt. A. Pushpavalli in her paper, "A study on the trend in growth of co-operatives in Tamilnadu with special reference to Primary Agricultural Credit Socieities." Presents with the help of statistical tools the trend of growth of co-operatives, membership, working capital etc.

The paper entitled, "Role of Co-operatives in Financing Agriculture" by Dr. R. N. Mishra focuses the flow of credit to the agriculturistis, term-wise supply of agricultural credit, mode of borrowing etc. in the district of Ganjam (Orissa).

Prof. Raghuraman Narayan in his paper outlines the co-operative movement in southern districts of Tamil Nadu. The primary agricultural co-operatives, consumer co-operatives, handloom co-operatives etc. have been presented with their recent policy indicators.

Prof. Rengaswamy and Dr. Mani in their joint paper, 'Co-operative Audit in Tamil Nadu' defines the meaning and needs of co-operative audit. Organisational structure, Role of the Director and Joint-director in the co-operative Audit, Powers of the co-operative auditors, etc. have been analysed in this paper.

Dr. S. N. Tripathy in his paper presents the role of LAMPS for the development of tribals of Orissa, based on secondary sources of data. The flow of credit, position of overdues both short-term and long-term, marketing of SAP during the period 1989 to 1994 have been analysed to draw some meaningful findings.

In their joint paper Prof. Pandey and Prof. J.P. Mishra have assessed the role of co-operative development corporation and fishery sector, etc.

Presenting the role of handloom sector in the economic development of weavers, the paper entitled, "Evaluating Primary Handloom Weavers' Co-operative Societies" by Sri R.K. Panda. Studies the percentage share of profit/loss making PHWCs, the production trend of

PHWCs, the price-behaviour and material cost index of the PHWCs in Ganjam district of Orissa.

Prof. Pandian and Ms. J. J. Rani studied the socio-economic status of co-operative handloom weavers of Tamil Nadu state with the help of sample questionnaire method.

The research write-up entitled, "Marketing of Handloom Fabrics by Co-optex in Tamil Nadu" by Prof. Rengaswamy & Mr. Jabarullahan points out the marketing problems, variety-wise procurement of fabrics by Co-optex and channels of distribution of handloom products in Tamil Nadu.

With the help of structured schedules administered to 150 buyers of silk sarees, the study made by Prof. (Mrs.) Pandian and Mrs. Felcitas brings into light various aspects of buyers of silk-sarees and their socio-economic features.

Thus, the present volume touches the multi-dimensional aspects of co-operatives in India with the help of research studies and their findings in various secotrs of co-operatives in our country. Before we conclude, it is appropriate to mention that both the leadership and the officials of the co-operative department should devote greater attention and imagination for perspective planning. It will be then possible for co-operatives to secure their due place in the programmes for bringing about socio-economic changes in the rural areas.

In fact, the present volume could not have been brought to light without the contribution of papers by the eminent professors and researchers. The editor expresses his deepest gratitude to all the paper contributors whose papers have enriched this volume.

I must acknowledge the help and encouragements, I have received from my wife Meera Rani, without whose co-operation it would have remained a dream unfulfilled. I owe a special debt to my son Sameer and daughter Sumita, who remained deprived of my love and affection during the period of editing the work.

Finally, I hope that the book will be immensely useful in guiding the policy makers, planners, researchers and persons engaged for the well-being of the public in various co-operative organisations and in formulating policy for the development of rural economy through strengthening the sources of institutional inance and expanding the dimensions of co-operatives in the non-credit spheres.

Author

Contents

1

Role of Industrial Cooperatives in the Context of New Industrial Policy for Rural and Urban Development

*Prof. (Dr.) K. Sain**

I

This exercise has three main objectives: First, to examine the nature of India's New Industrial Policy briefly. Secondly, to dwell on the economic roles of industrial cooperatives within the periphery of a private enterprise economy undergoing a process of planned economic development. Thirdly, to review the progress, economic potentiality and limitations of India's industrial cooperatives under the overall rural and urban developed plans of the country.

II

Secondary date contained in the Reports of the Departments of Cooperative of different Governments at home and abroad and of different local, national and international bodies are analysed to draw conclusions and to fulfil the objectives at hand through tabular presentation and use of recognised economic criteria.

III

The basic idea behind the New Industrial policy adopted by the present Government of India is to restructure and open the economy to free forces of competition, to the extent possible, at home and abroad to enable it to draw vigor and energy from entrepreneurs and investors

* Professor, Bidhan Chandra Krishi Viswavidyalaya, Department of Agricultural Economics, Kalyani (West Bengal).

from all sources—internal and external, while maintaining Government control and vigilance, ultimately, on essential and indispensable spheres only in the economy. This is expected to generate an immense opportunity for individual initiative and for cooperative ventures to contribute their full time at local, national and international forums for the accelerated growth and uplift of the industries in particular and of the economy in general.

The specific aspects of India's New Industrial policy and related economic reforms are : (i) Opening all areas of investment except 8 strategic and security areas (instead of earlier 17) to private sector. (ii) Elimination of industrial licensing of 80 p.c. of industry and except for 18 items. (iii) Removal of restrictions on location of industries except for 23 cities with more than 1 mn. people and subject to norms for environmental safety. (iv) Shift of emphasis from size of farms and investment to unfair, or monopolistic practices in applying Monopolistic and Restrictive Trade Practices Act irrespective of public, private, or, international ownership to boost production and efficiency at home. (v) Removal of law enabling financial institutions to take over management of firms by converting their loans into shares. (vi) A Foreign Investment Promotion Board has been set up to encourage use of more efficient foreign technologies and foreign collaboration and to allow remittance of dividend on foreign investment in foreign currencies outside India in case costs of such technologies and collaboration are covered by foreign equity with provision for even automatic approval by the Reserve Bank of India fur such efforts. (vii) Investment limits for small-scale and tiny industrial sectors have been raised upto Rs. 50 lakhs, e.g. this limit has been increased from Rs. 2 lakhs to Rs. 5 lakhs for export oriented plants and machineries. Large-scale industrial units have been permitted to hold shares in small-scale units upto 24 pc. of such holdings in the units. These are special incentives for the growth of these small industrial sectors. (viii) Private sector is encouraged to participate in infrastructural development: power, transport and communication on remunerative terms. (ix) States are encouraged to formulate and declare their own industrial policy by the centre. (x) A National Renewal Fund is being set up to retain and to redeploy the staff which may be rendered surplus as a result of deregulation and implementation of the N.I.P. (xi) Trade policy is being liberalised with introduction of Exit Scrip (30-40 p.c. of value of exports is given to the exporter in the form of marketable Exim scrips), system of open general Licence in most goods freely tradeable internationally, etc.

(xii) Disinvestment of shares of public sector industrial units and withdrawal of subsidies from them and for other purposes in general. (xiii) Off-loading of wheat by the Food Corporation of India and import of edible oils by the State Trading Corporation and strengthening of public distribution system, where necessary, to manage the price front well.

Already demand for industrial licenses declined sharply, e.g. from 3000 to 48 during 1991-92 over the correpsonding period of the earlier year. It is urgent that the spirit of cooperation is utilised to the fullest possible extent to reorganise and revitalize the small and tiny industrial sectors of the country under the N.I.P. for restructuring and opening the system to enterprise and competition.[1]

IV

Industrial cooperatives, the voluntary associations of people in handicraft, coir, sericulture, handloom and khadi and village industries in India and in such jobs elsewhere can play a valuable role in rural uplift and in economic revitalisation of a country in a number of ways: (i) To reduce uneconomic and excessive input and output levels margins of the inter-mediaries through a net-work of cooperative organisations (ii) To augment employment and income for their members by running plants for processing of farm products. (iii) to foster research and innovations for novel and quality products and for their easier and more profitable disposal. (iv) To increase bargaining power of their members through bulk and wiser handling of input and outputs. (v) To reduce per unit cost or production through efficient input combinations. (vi) To mobilise otherwise hidden resources for production and employment. (vii) To reduce concentration of means of production, to decentralize production and work centres and to redistribute wealth and income in favour of the weak and the poor and thus to prevent the private enterprise economy from destruction and ruin by serving as the golden mean between the extremes of capitalism and communism.

In the background of changing economic system towards a more liberalised and competitive form, the industrial cooperatives hold a good prospect for supplementing the economy, particularly at its weakest points.

V

In view of the fact that the industrial cooperatives are organisations of industrial units which are capital-light, labour-intensive and more

1. This and other natural numbers at the tops of words indicate serial numbers of references given at the end of this exercise.

employment generating, import-light, of low gestation period and of high fruition coefficiency, their presence is especially welcome in a developing economy best with the vicious circle of low income—low investment—low export—high unemployment. For instance, the industrial coops. (other than handloom) could offer employment to 8.33 lakh persons during 1972-73 in India as a whole. The handloom industrial coops. engaged 27 mn. weavers and turned out products worth Rs. 3500 crores during 1984-85 (with respective projected estimates of 3.6 mn. persons and output worth Rs. 5400 crores for 1989-90)[3]. Coir industries of India offered employment to 5.75 lakh persons during 1983-84.[3] The Khadi and village industries of India gave full-time and part-time jobs to 12.48 lakh and 25.41 lakh persons during 1984-85. Net value of their output was Rs. 381.57 crs. in 1984-85 in India.[2]

The worthwhileness of cooperative endeavor for utilisation of scarce resources of the country in generating supply of different essential items and thereby more income and employment for the masses at decentralised levels may be assessed from the substantially positive rates of production per rupee of net disbursement in Khadi and Village industries of India the ratios for the Khadi, Village industries and for Khadi and Village industries combined maintaining respectively at around 0.60, 4.00 and 2.00 over the years : 1975-76—1984-85 which exceeds the assumed productivity ratio of 1:4 for the projected annual growth rate for G.D.P. of 5.6 p.c. for the Eighth Five year Plan (1992-1997) of India, the growth rate being the product of saving- income ratio (assumed saving income ratio of India for the Eight Five Year Plan is 21.5 p.c) and productivity or of Incremental Capital Output ratio : ICOR)[5]. To be more explicit, the realised productivity ratio of the Khadi and the Village industries of India during 1975-76—1984-85 of 2:1 far exceeds the productivity ratio of the Seventh, Plan of 1:4, or the assumed even productivity ratio of India's Eight Plan (ICOR=4:1).[4] These estimates demonstrate the potentialities of the industrial coops. in the field of light and rural industries for vigorously supplementing industrial and economic upliftment programmes of India under its broad economic plans and spirited guidance. It may be mentioned that the Khadi and Village Industries Commission of India which has under its care besides Khadi (cotton, woolen and silk) 28 village industries implements development programmes of these industries through 27 State Khadi & Village Industries Boards, 1127 registered institutions and over 31000 Cooperative societies. The KVIC disbursed different amounts of funds for these industries for their operation. For the year: 1984-85, e.g., the total net disbursement to these industries was Rs. 467.44 crs. and value of their total production was Rs. 964.68 crs. resulting in production per rupee of net disbursement at 2.06, with obvious limitations in comparing this ratio with the productivity ratios of India's Five Year Plan, the estimated ratio of production per rupee of net disbursement by the KVIC serving only as a gross indicator of resource use efficiency.[2]

The detailed estimates of production per rupee of net disbursement by KVIC to the Khadi and Village Industries of India are given in Table 1.1 below.

Industrial cooperatives, however, suffer from a number of weaknesses including paucity of trained staff, want of adequate resources, lack of synchronisation between the input delivery systems and the output marketing systems. irregularity in loan repayment, inadequate protection against organised and large industries not-withstanding provision for some reservation by the Government, internal rivalry of members and excessive external intervention. As a result, industrial co-operatives become nonviable, non-functioning or, dormant and fail to deliver the goods. For example, the number of active industrial coops (excluding handloom) declined from 18195 in 1966-67 to 10300 in 1975-76 in India. In June, 1973, only 4214 out of a total of 12460 handloom coops. of India were in profit. For the State of West Bengal, of its 1095 industrial, coops of all types, only 571 are now functioning and the rest (48 p.c.) are non-functioning dormant societies. A total of 271205 industrial units were sick/weak in March 1995 in India of which 92.4 p.c. were non-viable. This phenomenon of non-viability and dormancy and industrial coops. warrant strong measures for their resuscitation, especially, in the context of changed economic situation under the new industrial policy of India.

It is suggested that an intensive investigation be conducted into the actual conditions of working of the industrial coops. immediately, that the active participation of their members be enlisted and assured through provision for individual incentives for marked contribution, that a congenial work environment be created where members get impetus to work on their own and not simply as an army of uniformed and that due stress be given on research and innovations in the spheres of production and marketing so that the industrial coops. really fit themselves to the genius of the nation and its dynamic industrial policy for a balanced rural-urban regeneration.

Table 1.1
Production/Rupee of Net Disbursement of Funds by Khadi & Village Industries Commission of India for the Khadi & Village Industries under Its Care : Productivity Ratios (Output : Capital , or, O/e)

(Rupees)

Sl. No. Industry	1975–76	1976–77	1977–78	1978–79	1979–80	1980–81	1981–82	1982–83	1983–84	1984–85
I. Khadi	0.59	0.65	0.63	0.60	0.59	0.60	0.60	0.64	0.64	0.60
II. Village Industries :										
1. Processing of Cereals, pulses & masalas	3.59	3.61	3.28	3.31	3.57	3.96	4.50	4.73	5.19	5.30
2. Ghani oil	3.71	3.72	3.42	3.96	4.00	4.59	5.13	5.16	5.60	5.75
3. Village leather	3.86	3.98	3.71	3.39	3.32	3.41	3.88	4.06	4.38	4.18
4. Cottage match	0.60	0.42	--	7.20	7.48	4.94	3.60	2.09	2.31	1.75
5. Cane gur & Khandsari	15.03	16.13	11.74	9.72	17.00	20.47	14.81	13.21	12.23	9.82
6. Palm gur & other palm products	3.54	3.43	3.78	4.41	4.62	4.72	5.00	5.32	5.71	6.98
7. Non-edible oils & soap	1.41	1.07	1.06	1.05	1.49	1.79	1.81	1.71	1.82	1.99
8. Handmade popen	1.10	1.05	1.11	1.36	0.64	0.68	1.31	1.09	0.90	0.88
9. Beekeeping	6.70	5.33	6.26	6.37	5.84	7.30	6.96	5.66	3.93	4.38
10. Village pottery	2.00	2.25	2.23	2.25	2.20	2.34	2.45	2.75	2.65	2.74

(Contd...)

Table 1.1 : (Contd.)

Sl. No.	Industry	1975–76	1976–77	1977–78	1978–79	1979–80	1980–81	1981–82	1982–83	1983–84	1984–85
11.	Fibre	6.41	6.43	6.34	5.77	6.21	5.69	5.62	5.35	4.69	4.89
12.	Carpentry & Blacksmithy	3.42	3.22	3.30	3.11	2.95	3.18	3.97	3.77	3.91	3.65
13.	Lime manufacturing	2.20	2.22	2.12	2.97	3.63	2.27	3.34	3.38	3.27	3.15
14.	Gobar (methane) gas	5.08	6.99	7.13	8.40	8.48	9.33	10.21	8.19	7.90	4.58
15.	New Industries	1.83	1.83	2.16	2.21	2.89	2.32	2.28	2.05	1.30	1.59
	Overall : II	3.71	3.74	3.59	3.64	4.11	4.24	4.19	4.01	4.13	3.97
	Overall : I+II	1.63	1.72	1.65	1.64	1.83	1.96	1.97	2.01	2.10	2.06

Note : (i) In processing of cereals and pulses, the calculation has been done on its total production, both commercial and non-commercial paddy, cereals and pulses.

(ii) Ratios do not include bank finance.

Source of basic data : Khadi & village Industries Commission : Annual Report : 1984–85. Bombay : 1986 : pp. 63–64.

References :

1) Dey, B. Industrial Cooperative in West Bengal : An Integrated Approach for Development : 1992 (Mimeo).

2) Khadi & Village Industries Commission - Annual Report : 1984-85, Bombay—1986.

3) National Institute of Rural Development : Rural Development Stastistics : Hyderabad : 1985.

4) Rangarajan, C. Contours of Eighth Plan ; *Yojana* : Vol. 36, No. 9. May 31 1992.

5) Sain, K. Technique of Planning for Agricultural Development of India. *Southern Economist* : Annual Number. Vol. 14. No. 1 & 2, May 1975.

6) Yojana : Economic Refortms : Some Aspects . *Yojana* : Vol. 36 No. 9, May 31, 1992.

7) Reserve Bank of India. Rerport on Trend and Progress of Banking in India : 1995-96 (July-June). Bombay : 1997. p-128.

2

Credit and its Use in Technological Development of Agriculture : Some Findings

*Satyendra P. Gupta**

Today, agriculture is becoming capital intensive in nature since the use of difference type of agricultural inputs like HYV seeds, fertilizers, plant protection material and machineries etc. require high expenditure. Undoubtedly, the recent technology and scientific advancement in agriculture has increased the income of some of the farm families, however, most of the marginal and small farmers are unable to meet this high expenditure in agriculture.

Though, several commercial banks have increased their scale of operation in rural areas to make available this high expenditure in terms of credit to these farmers, however, cooperative banks play very significant role in the rural economy through its Primary Agricultural Credit Societies (PACS). This cooperative credit (cash and kind) would not only helpful to adopt the capital intensive modern farm technology at these farms but also improved the economic condition of these farmers by raising the agricultural productivity.

In the same context, the present study is undertaken with the following specific objectives:

1. The extent and trends of cooperative credit in different purpose of agricultural sector,
2. Utilization pattern of cooperative credit at different categories of farms and

* Assistant Professor, Departmnet of Agricultural and Natural Resource Economics, Indira Gandhi Agricultural University, Krishak Nagar, Raipur—492 012 (M.P.)

3. The affect of cooperative credit on crop technology and income at different categories of sampled borrowers.

METHODOLOGY

The District Cooperative Bank, Raipur was purposively selected for the present study. The jurisdiction of the bank is whole district consisting 3850 villages in eleven tehsils in which bank is operating through its 51 branches. Among of these tehsils, Raipur tehsil was selected purposively since maximum financing was done in this tehsil (Table 2.1). Out of four blocks in this tehsil, Dharsiwa block was considered randomly for the present study. Among of three branches of District Cooperative Bank is this block, Ganj branch was taken into consideration since maximum credit was distributed by this branch through its fourteen PACS. Of this number, three PACS (20 percent) namely Datranga, Kachana and Sejbahar were included as these three PACS have financed more than 34 percent of the total credit financed by the Ganj branch of District Cooperative Bank.

Two villages (six in all) from each of the PACS were taken into consideration to take a sample of 36 borrowers (six from each village) in order to examine the utilization pattern of cooperative credit of different categories of the borrowers. These farmers were also asked about the crop technology used by them and the income from the crops enterprise. A sample of 24 non-borrowers (four from each village) was also considered randomly in order to compare the crop technology and income at both type (borrowers and non-borrowers) of farms. These farmers were classified into small (upto 2 ha) and medium (2.01 ha. to 4.00 ha.) on the basis of land holdings of the farmers. The analysis was made for each category separately for both type of farmers. The all information collected from these farmers were relate to year 1993-94.

RESULTS AND DISCUSSION

Extents and Trends in Cooperative Credit

Table 2.1 exhibits the extent of short term and mid term credit, financed to the small and large family in different tehsils of the district. As it is clear from the table, the ratio of midterm credit to total credit was not only negligible but also decreased drastically from Rs. 35.53 lakh in 1991-92 to Rs. 12.63 lakh in 1994-95. (Table 2.2). This sharp decline of mid term credit in agriculture is the area of serious concern because it would directly affect the capital formation in agriculture.

According to the economic survey (1993-94) the problem of investment in agriculture is not a problem of total availability of resource with the government but the distribution between the current expenditure in the form of increased level of subsidies for fertilizer, irrigation and electricity etc. and capital formation. It is high time that the investment in agriculture should be stepped up through the project approach. This would not only help in aiding the technology transfer through credit support but also encourage new and wider areas of activities.

Table 2.2 shows the trend in the flow of cooperative credit in agriculture sector from 1991–92 to 1994–95. It clearly reveals the fact that the short term cooperative credit have increased much faster (i.e. Rs. 937 lakh in 1991–92 to Rs. 5008 lakh in 1994–95) during a period of four years. The credit in form of cash has increased by 573 percent as maximum followed by 534 percent in case of fertilizer during the same period. Though, the credit for HYV seed has also increased by 234 percent, however, the credit for plant protection material has not shown comparable increase during the referred period of study. These figures strengthen the fact of need to increase the level of inputs in agriculture. This expenditure would not only raise the income of farmers by increasing the crop productivity but would also check the flow of labour from farm to non-farm sector by generating additional employment in agriculture.

As compared to short term credit, mid term credit has shown a drastic decline in all the cases except credit for dairying. Though, there is a serious problem of overdues which has been inhibiting mid term credit expansion and economic viability of the lending institutions specially the cooperative, however, for a better flow of mid and long term agricultural credit, it is necessary that the scattered lending is replaced by a projectised and purposive lending and commercialization of agriculture through establishing a good infrastructure at farm level. The banks in India should reorient their conventional mode of financing to provide more funds for innovative activities like drip irrigation, soil conservation sericulture, horticulture, tissue culture, forestry and aquaculture in which high potential is there is enhance the productivity in agriculture sector.

Socio-Economic Profile of Farmers

Socio-economic profile of sample farmers is presented in Table 2.3. As evident from the table, leased-in land was quite more at small farms of borrowers and non-borrowers as compared to medium farmers. It was observed during the course of study that most of the small farmers had some surplus family labour which were in search of work. The tendency of taking leased-in land helps these farmers to work at their fields during the kharif season. This fact is strengthen with the number of adult member per hectare of cultivable land which was more than 2.63 at both type of small farms while this number was less than 2 at medium farms. Though, in kharif season almost all area was under paddy cultivation at borrowers and non-borrowers farms but area under rabi was relatively higher at borrowers farms. The cropping intensity was also observed quite higher i.e. 165 percent at small farms and 156 percent at medium farms of borrowers as compared to non-borrowers where it was 142.07 percent and 126.56 percent respectively.

Utilisation Pattern of Co-operative Credit

The utilization of credit finance by Cooperative Bank to the farmers is given in Table 2.4. The short term credit and mid term credit were observed to be 57.15 per cent and 42.85 per cent respectively. Though, the amount of short term credit was quite low (Rs. 2049.50) at small farms than medium (Rs. 5757.75), the percentage to the total credit at these farms was observed to be higher as compared to medium farms. On the contrary, the percentage of mid term credit was estimated as 48.16 per cent at medium farms which was relatively higher than 33.25 per cent at small farms. The per hectare utilization of short term credit at medium farms (Rs. 1810.61) was not much higher than per hectare utilization at small farms (Rs. 1652.82), however, per hectare utilization of mid term credit at medium farm was estimated more than double i.e. Rs. 1682.39 as compared to per hectare utilization (Rs. 823.25) of same kind of credit at small farms.

Total kind credit was provided in the form of fertilizer while whole short term cash provided to farmers, was spent by them to pay for hired labour, tractor and purchase for plant protection material and fertilizer. More than 70 per cent money of total short term cash was utilised to pay for hiring the labour by the farmers. Generally, farmers have spent more than 90 per cent of mid term credit to purchase the drought animals while rest of the money was spent to purchase the milch animals. The outstanding mid term credit was found to be 34.81 per cent at medium farms only. The percentage of overdues in cash of short term credit was observed to be 13.52 per cent and 5.55 per cent at small and medium farms respectively.

Impact of Cooperative Credit

Table 2.5 shows the impact of cooperative credit on crop technology and income of the borrowers. As evident from the table, 19.44 percent area of total paddy cultivation was allocated under HYV at the medium farms of borrowers which was considerably higher than 5.2 per cent at the non-borrowers of the same category. Area under transplanting has direct relation with the size of holding of farms of borrowers. This methods was not adopted at non-borrowers farms. A big difference was recorded in the use of fertilizer at both type of farms. It was estimated as 241.18 kg./hectare at borrowers farms which was 64 per cent more as compared to use of fertiliser by non-borrowers. This high use of fertilizer in the study area was observed as the District Cooperative Bank preferred to sanction the credit largely in the form of kind component subject to better utilization of the credit.

The crop income was estimated to be Rs. 8970.97 and Rs. 21259.20 at small and medium farms of borrowers respectively which was about 88 per cent and 119 per cent more as compared to the income at same categories of non-borrowers. The high productivity of crop due to higher level of inputs of borrower's farm seems to be a possible reason for this high crop income at these farms. The per hectare crop income was computed as Rs. 5642.12 and Rs. 6561.48 at small and medium farms of borrowers while it was Rs. 2898.76 and Rs. 3180.14 only at same categories of non-borrowers. The higher level use of different inputs like fertilizer and plant protection material alongwith improved method of cultivation followed by the borrowers seems to be an important reason of this more than double income as compared to non-borrowers.

Conclusion

The study has shown that the ratio of mid term credit in total credit was not only negligible in the district but also decreased drastically from Rs. 35.33 lakh in 191-92 to Rs. 12.63 lakh in 1994-95. On the other side, the short term cooperative credit was increased much faster i.f. from RS. 937 lakh to RS. 5008 lakh during the same period of four years. The short term credit in the form of cash and fertilizer has increased more than five folds during last four years.The per hectare utilization of short-term credit at medium farm (Rs.1810.61) was not much higher than per hectare utilization at small farms (Rs. 1652.82), however, per hectare utilization of mid term credit at medium farm was estimated more than double i.e. Rs. 1682.39 than per hectare utilization of same kind of credit at small farms. Though, the improved crop technology in the form of HYV seeds, transplanting, fertilizer and plant protection material was observed considerably higher at borrowers farms, however, it is necessary to adopt it adequately in order to further improve the productivity of the crops. The per farm crop income at borrowers farm was estimated as RS. 13067.05 which was about 104.09 per cent more than the income (Rs. 6402.45) of non-borrowers. Due to higher level use of different inputs by the borrowers, they experienced more than double per hectare income as compared to non-borrowers.

Table 2.1 : Credit Distribution by District Co-operative Bank, Raipur in Raipur District of Madhya Pradesh

Tehsils	*Small Farmers (Below 4 ha.)*			*Large Farmers (Above 4 ha.)*		
	Short Term	*Mid Term*	*Total*	*Short Term*	*Mid Term*	*Total*
Baloda Bazar	13738	4	13742 (10.64)	25377	21	25398 (10.94)
Bhata Para	2271	6	2277 (1.76)	5936	22	5958 (2.57)
Bilaigarh	3291	3	3294 (2.55)	4425	51	4476 (1.93)
Dhamtari	28074	38	28112 (21.76)	38478	141	38619 (16.64)
Gariyaband	4794	10	4804 (3.72)	8030	38	8068 (3.48)
Kasdol	3632	--	3632 (2.81)	5112	2	5114 (2.20)
Mahasamund	15462	26	15488 (11.99)	33729	559	34288 (14.78)
Raipur	36259	69	36328 (28.11)	58894	87	58981 (25.41)
Rajim	7928	501	8429 (6.52)	8796	9	8892 (3.83)
Saraipali	7724	45	7769 (6.01)	25067	1223	26290 (11.33)
Simga	5339	--	5339 (4.13)	15957	37	15994 (6.89)
District	128512	702	129214 (100.00)	229801	2277	232078 (100.00)

Note : Figures in the parenthesis indicate the percentages to total financing to the farmers.

Source : Based on block-wise information collected from District Cooperative Bank, Raipur

Table 2.2 : Purpose-wise Flow of Co-operative Credit in Agricultural Sector of Raipur District of Madhya Pradesh

(Rs. in lakh)

Purpose	*1991–92*	*1992–93*	*1993–94*	*1994–95*
Short Term Credit				
i) Cash	290.02 (100.00)	1435.56 (495.02)	1408.91 (485.83)	1660.99 (572.76)
ii) Seed	17.80 (100.00)	39.87 (223.99)	41.46 (232.92)	41.57 (233.54)
iii) Plant Protection material	11.90 (100.00)	7.37 (61.93)	12.03 (101.09)	13.57 (114.03)
iv) Fertilizers	616.91 (100.00)	2115.03 (342.84)	2506.73 (406.34)	3292.02 (533.63)
Total Short Term Credit	936.63 (100.00)	3597.81 (384.12)	3969.13 (423.77)	5008.15 (534.70)
Mid-Term Credit				
i) Milch animal	0.27 (100.00)	0.10 (37.03)	0.13 (48.15)	0.15 (55.56)
ii) Draft animal	9.79 (100.00)	1.43 (14.60)	3.10 (31.66)	3.26 (33.30)
iii) Agril. equipment	3.94 (100.00)	1.34 (34.01)	0.84 (21.32)	0.45 (11.42)
iv) Land improvement	0.92 (100.00)	0.73 (79.35)	0.34 (36.96)	0.19 (20.65)
v) Irrigation development	5.99 (100.00)	1.48 (24.71)	2.32 (38.73)	2.29 (38.23)
vi) Gobar Gas Plant	14.42 (100.00)	24.43 (169.42)	12.23 (80.81)	6.29 (43.62)
vii) Poultry	---	3.20 (100.00)	2.06 (64.38)	---
viii) Dairy	---	0.10 (100.00)	1.06 (1060.00)	---
Total mid-term credit	35.33 (100.00)	32.81 (92.87)	22.08 (62.50)	12.63 (35.75)
Total Credit	971.96 (100.00)	3630.62 (373.54)	3991.21 (410.64)	5020.78 (516.56)

Note : Figures in the parenthesis indicate the credit index number.

Source : Computed from data collected from District Co-operative Bank, Raipur, M.P.

Table 2.3 : Socio-economic Profile of the Sampled Farmers

(Area in hectare/farm)

Particulars	*Borrowers*			*Non-Borrowers*		
	Small	*Medium*	*Aggregate*	*Small*	*Medium*	*Aggregate*
Sample households (No.)	24	12	36	16	8	24
Farm size	1.25	3.18	1.89	1.12	2.90	1.71
Leased-in land	0.34	0.06	0.24	0.52	0.15	0.40
Total cultivate land	1.59	3.24	2.13	1.64	3.05	2.11
Total fragments (No.)	2.42	4.25	3.03	2.38	3.75	2.83
Kh. Irrigated land	1.26 (79.25)	2.86 (88.27)	1.79 (83.64)	1.46 (89.02)	2.49 (81.64)	1.80 (85.31)
Area under Kh.	1.59	3.24	2.13	1.64	2.82	2.03
Area under rabi	1.02 (64.55)	1.84 (56.79)	1.29 (60.28)	0.69 (42.07)	1.04 (34.10)	0.81 (38.39)
Cropped Area	2.61	5.08	3.42	2.33	3.86	2.84
Cropping Intensity (percent)	165.18	156.00	161.03	142.07	126.56	134.60
Family size (No.)	8.25	13.42	9.97	9.27	10.87	9.80
Adult Members (No.)	4.16	6.41	4.91	4.62	5.63	4.96
Members working in agriculture	3.46	5.58	4.17	3.81	4.63	4.08
Adult Members (No. per ha.)	2.63	1.98	2.31	2.82	1.85	2.35

Note : Figures in the parenthesis indicate the percentages to total cultivable land.

Table 2.4 : Utilization of Credit Financed by Co-operative Bank at Sampled Farms of Borrowers

(Rs. in lakh)

Particulars	Small	Medium	Aggregate
A. Short Term Credit			
i) Kind	1512.00	4049.42	2357.80
ii) Cash	537.50	1708.33	927.78
	2049.50 (66.75)	5757.75 (51.84)	3285.58 (57.15)
Loan utilized (Rs./ha.)	1652.82	1810.61	1747.65
Utilization of Cash			
i) To purchase the pl. protection material	23.32	153.75	66.81
ii) To hire the tractor	90.00	200.00	126.67
iii) To pay for hired labour	380.48	1331.58	697.51
iv) To purchase fertilizers	43.70	23.00	36.79
Outstanding loans	415.25 (13.52)	616.67 (5.55)	482.39 (8.39)
B. Mid-term Credit			
	1020.83 (33.25)	5350.00 (48.16)	2463.89 (42.85)
Loan utilized (Rs./ha.)	823.25	1682.39	1310.58
Utilization of Cash			
i) To purchase draught animals	833.25	5350.00	2338.89
ii) To purchase milch animals	187.50	---	125.00
Outstanding loans	---	3866.67 (34.81)	1288.89 (22.42)
Total Loans	3070.33 (100.00)	11107.75 (100.00)	5749.47 (100.00)

Note : Figures in the parenthesis indicate the percentages to total loan given to the farmers.

Table 2.5 : Impact of Co-operative Credit on Crop Technology and Income of the Borrowers

(Quantity in kg./ha.)
(*Area in hectare/farm*)
(Income in Rs.)

Particulars	*Borrowers*			*Non-Borrowers*			
	Small	*Med-ium*	*Aggre-gate*	*Small*	*Med-ium*	*Aggre-gate*	% change
A. Crop Technology :							
Area under HYV	0.29 (18.24)	0.63 (19.44)	0.40 (18.69)	0.30 (18.29)	0.15 (5.32	0.25 (12.25)	+60.00
Area under trans-planting	0.16 (10.06)	0.53 (16.36)	0.28 (13.08)	--- --	--- --	--- --	+100.00
Use of fertilizer	234.89	253.77	241.18	143.72	153.00	146.81	+64.28
Use of plant protection material	3.32	4.42	3.68	2.57	2.91	2.68	+37.31
Crop area (ha.)	2.61	5.08	3.43	2.33	3.86	2.84	+20.77
Area under paddy	1.59	3.24	2.14	1.64	2.82	2.04	+4.90
B. Crop Income :							
i) Kharif	8288.91	18728.53	11768.78	4590.37	9022.97	6067.90	+93.95
ii) Rabi	682.06	2530.67	1298.27	163.59	676.45	334.55	+288.06
Crop Income	8970.97	21259.20	13067.05	4753.96	9699.42	6402.45	+104.09
Income (Rs./ha.)	5642.12	6561.48	6134.77	2898.76	3180.14	2099.16	+192.25

Note : Figures in the parenthesis indicate the percentages to total area under paddy.

References

Bhat, N.S. (1995), Agricultural Borrowers from Banks : A Profile and Policy Implication, Financing Agriculture Vol. XXVII No. 2 pp. 15–19.

Desai, D.K. (1988), Institutional Credit Requirement for Agricultural Production 2000 A.D., IJAE, Vol. 43, pp. 326–355.

District Coop. Bank, District Credit Plan, 1992–93, Raipur.

Gupta, S.P. (1994), Possibilities of Agril. Development Through Coop. Finance : An Analytical Study Financing Agriculture Vol. XXVI No. 3 pp. 8–13.

Parihar R. S. and Singh N. (1988), A Study into Institutional Finance for the Agricultural Sector in Punjab, IJAE, Vol. 43 (3) pp. 381–389.

Patel, P. M. (1988), Integrated Approach to Institutional Finance for Agriculture : A Case Study of Three Co-op. Societies in Sabarkantha District of Gujrat, IJAE, Vol. 43, (3) pp. 390–397.

Rao, G.V.K., (1994), Speech at the twenty-sixth Annual General Meeting of Agricultural Finance Corporation, Vol. XXVI, (3), pp. 25–28.

Singh Ranveer et. al. (1995) Agricultural Credit Overdues : Emerging Problems in Himachal Pradesh, Financing Agriculture Vol. XXVII No. 1 pp. 4–9.

3

Farm Credit and Non-farm Credit Recovery Performance of Karatadipalayam Primary Agricultrual Co-operative Bank Ltd., Erode District

Dr. S. Lakshmanan*

Co-operative is an instrument for accelerating economic development particularly in developing countries like India. It removes disparities is the distribution of income and wealth. The essence of co-operative principles lies in (a) Democratic association (Democracy); (b) Voluntary participation (voluntaryism) (c) Autonomous control (autonomy); (d) Equitable distribution (equity); (e) Mutual motivation (mutuality); (f) universal integration (universality); and (g) Voluntary growth (evolution).

The co-operative societies are very important organ in performing various functions needed for quick economic growth. The Reserve Bank of India classified Co-operative Society as follows:

(1) Co-operative banking structure which includes agricultural credit societies, large-sized societies, rural banks, central co-operative banks, State Co operative banks, central land mortgage banks, primary land mortgage banks and urban credit.

(2) Co-operative as an aid to production, which includes agricultural and allied production and industrial production.

(3) Co-operative marketing including primary marketing societies, central marketing societies, state mortgage societies, national

* Reader in Economics, Gobi Rural Arts and Science College (Autonomous) Erode District, Tamilnadu (India)—638 453

agricultural co-operative marketing federation, sugarcane supply societies, processing societies and co-operative sugar factories.

4) Other forms of cooperation, namely, consumer's stores, housing societies, workers co-operatives, women's co-operatives, displaced persons co-operative societies and insurance cooperation.

In a developing country like India, rural savings are larger, and this can be mobilised easily by means of rural co-operative society. The principle of co-operation can be used in the filed of agricultural and non agricultural sector. It enhances the agricultural productivity, industrial productivity and proper distribution of goods. It also brings equal distribution of income and wealth, employment opportunities, development of infrastructure and finally induces globalization of economic forces. Therefore the principle of co-operation is inevitable force in the dynamic economic and social development of modern societies.

Agriculture is an important industry and like other industries. It also requires capital. Due to the peculiarities of agriculture, specially, its uncertainties, its small unit production, scattered operation, low returns high rates of rent and limited scope of employment, a large proportion of cultivators cannot manage from one harvest to another without recourse to borrowings. Sir, F.A. Nicholson stated in his monumental report, "The history of rural economy, alike in Europe, America and India, has no less or more distinct than this, that agriculturist must and will borrow. The necessity is due to the fact that an agriculturist's capital is locked up in this land stock, and must be temporarily mobilised, hence credit is neither necessarily objectionable nor is borrowing necessarily a sign of weakness"

The development of institutional credit is thus, a basic condition for agricultural progress. The history of agricultural development in all advanced countries shows that an integrated system of institutional credit laid the foundation of agricultural prosperity. The objectives of the institutional credit is to make a breakthrough in the vicious circle of poverty, reck-renting, usury and debt and to stimulate the farmer to boost agricultural productivity. This would mean in the words of Dr. Horace Belshaw "the conversion of static into dynamic credit".

These institutional arrangements are expected to do the following functions:

Facilities and encourage savings and mobilization for productive investments, reduce the cost of credit, administration; pool the risks of lenders; increase competition between private money lenders and effectively counter the local monopolies which many of them now enjoy.

Credit can be classified period-wise, purpose-wise, security-wise creditor-wise. The term of period of the loan is the most commonly accepted classification. According to it credit is classified as short-term, medium-term and long-term.

Short-Term Credit

Short-term credit is given for seasonal agricultural operations directed towards raising of crop on land, including a reasonable amount for the maintenance needs of the farmer and his family Short-term loans are generally made for 12 months. They are given for purchasing seeds, manure and fertilizers or for meeting labour charges, etc., and are to be repaid after the harvest.

In the words of All India Rural Credit Review Committee, the short-term credit is "a kind of lump-sum accommodation to fill up the gaps in outlay which cannot be met from the cultivator's own resources during the non-income period between two harvests".

Medium-Terms Credit

The medium term loans are given a period ranging from over 12 months to 5 years for purposes such as reclamation of land, building and other land improvements, purchase of livestock, machinery and other implements, sinking of wells, constructions of pucca drains in the field etc.

Long-Term Credit

Long-Term Credit is given for period ranging between 5 to 20 years, for purposes such as the redemption of land, liquidation of debts, purchase of tractors and land and improvements of a permanent nature in land.

The primary Agricultural Credit Societies (PACS), also known as village credit societies were established in the country on the Raiffeisen mode. As Wolff observed: "It is the local society-the single brick at the bottom larger upon which the intended fabric has to rest-which makes for the safety of the organisation."

The primary agricultural credit societies which are the krnel of the co-operative movement are expected to undertake the major functions such as raising of adequate resources and supply of adequate and timely short and medium-term credit: supply of necessary inputs required for members undertake marketing of agricultural produce; supply of certain consumer goods and inculcate thrift and self help among the members.

Co-operative Banking

In India, commercial banks cater to the requirements of highly organised industry and commercial undertakings. The co-operative banks provide banking facilities to the unorganised agricultural sector of the country. The co-operative banks provide adequate supply of loans to the farming sector. A cooperative bank promotes economic activity and provides banking facilities and services to the rural people. Thrift and savings is the objective of the working of co-operative banks. Co-operative lending is the means to promote thrift and savings and services, and profit is not the chief motto. Personalization of credit is the special feature of the co-operative banking. In India, mechanisation of agriculture has been rapidly picking up. Therefore, the marginal, small, medium and big farmers need more agricultural finance. The co-operative banks provide short-term, medium-term and long-term loans to both agricultural and non-agricultural sector.

Agricultural Co-operatives are classified as:

a) Short term and Medium Term Institution.

b) Long term credit Institutions.

Under the short term and medium term institutions, we have State Co-operative banks, Central Co-operative Banks and Village Banks. Under long term credit institutions, we have Primary Land Development Banks. With regard to Non-agricultural banks, the following are important:

(1) Employees Credit Society

(2) Central Govt Urban Banks.

(3) Primary Co-operative Urban Bank

(4) Central Co-operative House Mortgage Banks.

(5) City Co-operative House Mortgage Banks.

(6) Apex Industrial Co-operative Banks.

(7) Primary Industrial Banks.

Tamilnadu is one of the leading states in India where co-operative societies have made rapid progress. It was the Madras Government which took the lead in establishing co-operative credit societies in placing Sir Fredrick Augustus Nicholson on special duty for the purpose of enquiring into the possibility of introducing land and agricultural banks.

With regard to development of Primary Agricultural Co-operative banks, the following achievements can be mentioned :

During the year 1997-98, short-term loans were issued to the tune of Rs. 697.99 Crores through 4589 PACBs in the state of 7.60 lakhs members.

Medium term loans were issued to the extent of Rs. 100.74 crores to 91,742 members. Out of the total short term and medium term loans issued during 1997-98, Rs. 519.44 crores were issued to weaker sections.

During the year 1998-99, target has been fixed to issue short term loans and medium term loans to the extent of Rs. 925 crores and Rs. 100 crores respectively.

It has been programmed to issue 67% of the short term loans and 95% of the medium term loans to the weaker sections during the year 1998-99.

Long term loans were issued to the extent of Rs. 191.40 crores to 27,800 members in the year 1997-98. It has been programmed to issue long term loans to the extent of Rs. 248.60 crores during 1998–99 through the Tamil Nadu Agricultural and Rural Development Bank.

Co-operative have issued jewel loans worth of Rs. 2779.97 crores during the last year. About 38.85 lakh members have benefitted. During the year 1998-99, target has been fixed to issue jewel loans to the tune of Rs. 3400 crores.

Under the non-farm sector loan scheme loans were issued to the extent of Rs. 93.94 crores during 1997-98 to 40,000 persons. It has been programmed to issue non-farm sector loans to the extent of Rs. 130 crores during 1998-99.

An Analysis Farm Credit and Non-Farm Credit—Recovery Performance of Karatadadipalayam Primary Agricultural Co-operative Bank Ltd., No. AA. 198

The Khusro Committee has rightly pointed out the recovery is main determinant in assessing the performance of co-operative credit structure. It is in this context that the present study has been undertaken by the author in order to assess the recovery position of both farm and non farm credit of Karatadi palayam Primary Agricultural Co-operative Bank. The bank is located in Erode District of Tamil Nadu State. This society was registered on 31.3.1957. The area of operations of the bank consist of kartadipalayam Village, Kalingayam Village and Ayalar Village. The functions of the society are:

1. To provide short-term and long term loans to the marginal and small and big farmers.
2. To provide agricultural inputs like fertilizer etc.
3. To provide non-farm credit like consumer credit and jewel loans to both to members and non members.

The Kartadipalayam Co-operative bank is purposively selected for the study due to the accessibility to data and familiarity with its service area. The data under investigation relates to co-operative years from 1986-87 to 1996-97. The required primary data for the study were collected from the audit reports, Annual reports, Loans registers etc., by personal visit. The tabular analysis has been used to analyse the data, the statical tools like percentage analysis and index numbers have been used.

Results and Discussion

a) Membership

The increasing membership is an indicator of growth of a society. The membership consist of A class (The value of share is Rs. 10), B Class (The Value of Shar is Rs. 5) and the State Government (1 Share). A class membership consist of persons residing on own lands in the area of operation of the bank and B class consists of individual availing gold loans, vehicle loans, consumer durables etc., Table 3.1 presents the membership details. The table reveals that the A class membership increase From 4103 in 1989 to 5169 in 1997. The index number of membership has increased 100 points in1987 to 125.98 points. With regard to B class membership the number rose from 1635 to 2150 in 1997 which is proved by index number.

b) Share Capital

From the Table 3.2, it is understood that the share capital of the society has increased from Rs. 3,20,260 in 1987 to Rs. 5,03769 in 1997. The index number shows an increasing trend i.e. from 100 point in 1987 to 157.30n in 1997. With regard to "B" class membership share, the index number shows an upward increase of share capital.

Table 3.1 : Membership Details

Year	Membership			
	A Class	Index No.	B Class	Index No.
1987	4103	100.00	1635	100.00
1988	4198	102.32	1781	108.93
1989	4180	101.88	1884	115.23
1990	4236	103.24	1968	120.37
1991	4348	105.97	2091	127.89
1992	4479	109.16	2091	127.89
1993	4994	121.72	2091	127.89
1994	5018	122.30	2091	127.89
1995	5009	122.08	2091	127.89
1996	5043	122.91	2150	131.49
1997	5169	125.98	2150	131.50

Table 3.2 : Share Capital

Year	Amount	Index No.
1987	320260	100.00
1988	400770	125.139
1989	421182	131.513
1990	480971	150.181
1991	464736	145.112
1992	491958	153.612
1993	494060	154.269
1994	476042	148.642
1995	457216	142.764
1996	432760	135.128
1997	503769	157.300

c) Investments

The society makes investment in various schemes. It makes investment in Periyar Central Co-operative Bank, Indira Vikas Patra, Kissan Vikas Patra and Buildings. As society has to withdraw the amount of capital invested in Periyar Central Co-operative Bank to give farm loans, to Marginal farmers, small farmers and consumer loans, the investment trends shows fluctuations as proved by index number. The data in Table 3.3 explains that the investments made by the society was poor in 1991.

Table 3.3 : Investment Details

Year	*Amount (Rs.)*	*Index No.*
1987	781644	100.00
1988	648270	82.94
1989	1148575	146.94
1990	1162751	148.76
1991	645319	82.56
1992	984490	125.95
1993	1433078	183.34
1994	1657568	212.06
1995	1589953	203.41
1996	1642600	210.15
1997	1429955	182.94

d) Deposits

The society receives the deposits from Porkadal Deposits, Fixed Deposits, Savings Deposit and Thrift Deposit. The volume of deposits collected by the society and index number of deposit is presented in the Table 3.4. It is clear from the table that the deposit index has increased from 100 points in 1987 to 372 points in 1997. It is evident from the data that the society has been more successful in mobilising the deposits.

An analysis of farm and Non Farm Credit Recovery

The society has an important objective of disbursing loans to members of the society. It provides short term credits, medium term credit and long term credit to farmers. The short term credit for one year (11.5% p.a.) medium term loan (12.5% p.a.) and long term loan (13.5%p.a.). The long term period is more than 5 years and less than 20 years. From the Table 3.5 it could be observed that in 1986, an amount of Rs. 1739695 has been distributed to the farmers. In 1995, the amount has been increased to Rs. 2919978/-. With reference to

Table 3.4 : Deposits Details

Year	Amount (Rs.)	Index No.
1987	1181727	100.000
1988	1650421	139.660
1989	2093888	177.189
1990	2035024	172.208
1991	2671884	226.099
1992	2673634	226.248
1993	2576797	218.053
1994	2719292	230.112
1995	2721492	230.298
1996	2723692	230.484
1997	4397602	372.133

recovery, the highest recovery has been established in the year 1987 (80.12%).

The lowest recovery witnessed in the year 1985 (33%). The reasons for higher recovery during the period have been (1) A good yield of agricultural production. (2) Effective official machinery in collecting overdues. (3) The reasonable rate of interest.

The reasons for lower recovery have been identified as follows: (1) The expectations of the farmers about the waiving policy of the Government. (2) Expected return is not available in agriculture due to failure of monson etc., (3) Political Pressures.

The average percentage of recovery with regard to farm credit has been 61.73%.

Non-Farm Credit Recovery Position :

Non farm credit is given by the society in the farm of consumer loans. The consumer loans include vehicle loan, consumer durables like T.V. Refrigerator etc. The non farm credit given by the society during the period 1986 to 1977 is presented in the Table 3.6. In 1986, an amount of Rs. 2080555/- has been issued. In 1994, a considerable amount of RS. 4848261/- has been issued. The lowest recovery has been witnessed in the year 1986 (54%). The highest recovery (91%) has been witnessed in the year 1997. The reason for higher recovery

Table 3.5 : Farm Credit Recovery

Year	*Sanctioned (Rs.)*	*Recovered (Rs.)*	*Index No.*
1986	1739695	1350831	77.65
1987	1947774	1560710	80.13
1988	1821232	1234062	67.76
1989	2185466	1861785	85.19
1990	2469110	1540150	62.38
1991	2572112	1716127	66.72
1992	2282340	1146367	50.23
1993	2418946	1273569	52.65
1994	2618940	1670168	63.77
1995	2919978	1117807	38.28
1996	1823827	1134743	62.22
1997	3674337	1243000	33.83

Table 3.6 : Non-Farm Credit Recovery

Year	*Sanctioned (Rs.)*	*Recovered (Rs.)*	*Index No.*
1986	2080555	1130625	54.34
1987	1902515	1231560	64.73
1988	2308050	1918241	83.11
1989	2244650	1615212	71.96
1990	2478210	1819600	73.43
1991	2762712	2218610	80.30
1992	2917735	2228110	76.36
1993	3015962	2015618	66.83
1994	4848261	3912414	80.70
1995	2206992	1802116	81.65
1996	4162712	3516280	84.47
1997	4284541	3912190	91.31

have been due to :

(1) The loan is given for employees to the society.

(2) The loan is repaid periodically because any default in the payment of loan will lead to additional interest.

(3) The salary class are mainly preferred for the issue of Consumer loans.

(4) Proper security is also taken into account while distributing the loans.

As compared to average farm credit recovery (61.73%), the non farm credit recovery has been higher (75.75%).

Conclusion

From the results the study, following conclusions could be arrived at:

1) The membership of the society shows an increasing trend.

2) With regard to deposits, the society gives a good performance.

3) With regard to share capital for "A" class members, it can be mentioned that there is higher growth of share capital during the period between 1987-1997.

4) With regard to farm credit recovery and non farm credit recovery the average percentage of non farm credit has been higher than the farm credit recovery. Therefore, the society is benefited out of non farm credit.

Hence, from the study, it may be suggested that the bank should place more emphasis on collecting the farm overdues with effective supervision. The bank must findout willful defaults and non-willful defaults. The fresh loan must be issued or existing loan may be extended only to those who repay the loan regularly. The problem seems to be less with regard to non repayment of non farm credit. Hence, the default in farm credit recovery must be taken care while assessing on performing of a co-operative credit institution.

References

1. T.N. Hajela "Co-operation Principles, Problems and Practice."

2. E.S. Bogbardu, "Principles of Co-operation"

3. Ashley Montague, "On Being Human", 1950, New York.
4. A.E. Emerson, "Science".
5. K.R. Kulkarni, "Theory and Practice of Co-operation in India and Broad, Vol.I".
6. "Agricultural Banker" Journal.
7. "The Tamilnadu journal of Co-operation" Journal
8. "Kotturavu" - Tamil Journal.
9. "R.B.I. Bulletion" - Journal.
10. "All India Rural Credit Review Committee - 1969" - Report.
11. "Report of the Committee on Co-operation in India - 1915"
12. "The administrative Repots & Audited records of Karatadipalayam Primary Agricultural Co-operative Bank Ltd.".

4

Co-operative Credit and Agricultural Development in Uttar Pradesh with Special Reference to Hamirpur District

Prof. J.P. Misra and*
*Shri Kumar Rawat***

The Co-operative Act was passed in 1904 on the pattern of Raiffeisen model in India on the basis of the report of Mr. F. Nicholson for the formation of credit societies to solve the problems of agricultural credit. But it was observed that progress of the co-operative societies was very poor because the Act did not provide provision for the formation of non-credit societies. Therefore, it was insufficient and hence, looking of the problem the Act was amended in 1912 and from the then remarkable progress has been made. The co-operation become provintial subject under the reform Act of 1919.

The co-operative structure is three-tier, comprises of primary societies at village level, in the field of credit and non-credit activities, central organisation at district level and an apex organisation at state level. The fundamental functions of Primary Agricultural Credit Societies (PACS) are to provide short and medium term credit to its members. The costs of inputs like seeds, fertilizers, pesticides, irrigational expenses are provided as short term and costs of live-stock, implements machineries, irrigational channel etc. as medium term by these organ-

* Professor of Agricultural Economics, N.D. University of Agriulcture & Technology, Kumarganj, Faizabad—224 229 (U.P.) India.

**Senior Research Fellow (Agril. Economics), N.D. University of Agriulcture & Technology, Kumarganj, Faizabad—224 229 (U.P.) India.

isations. The long-term credit are provided by the Co-operative Land Development Banks: Marketing of agricultural produce are also undertaken by the co-operatives to increase the income of the producers by providing them remunerative prices through efficient marketing system. NAFED is playing good role in this directions. A number of non-credit co-operative societies are also functioning in the country to provide the help to the weaker section of the societies. Thus, the main objectives of co-operatives is to increase the agricultural production of the members of co-operative societies and enable them to receive reasonable prices of their produce.

The development of co-operative societies can be divided into two stages; firstly, during 1950-60, the members of small co-operative societies were opened which increased the quantitative numbers of their societies. Secondly, after Patel Committee Report in 1961, the co-operative societies were re-organised. Though it decreased the number of co-operative societies and increased the qualitative of the co-operative societies. The numbers of co-operative societies were 44.08 lakhs in 1950-51, 170.40 lakhs in 1960-61 and 309.63 lakhs in 1970–71, which are at present about 812.39 lakhs.The deposits of co-operatives are also increased from Rs. 4.28 crores in 1950-51 to Rs. 26600 crores in 1980-81. Similarly the co-operative advances are also increased from Rs. 2290 crores in 1950-51 to Rs. 4200 crores in 1988–89.

No doubt, after nationalization of major bank on 19th July 1969 and after establishment of RRBs on 2nd Oct. 1975. these organisations are playing remarkable role for lending to agricultural sector but even then co-operatives are playing a vital role in agricultural financing. A multipurpose co-operative society in not only providing the credit to the members but also initiating for savings and providing essential items for their family needs. Thus, co-operative Act was passed to safeguard the interest of the members.

Co-operative movement in U.P. is started soon after the passing of cooperative Act in 1904, largely with a view to providing agricultural fund for agricultural operations at low rate of interest and protect them from clutches of money lenders, so that, the economic conditions of the farmers can be improved. A three tier scheme has been prepared for giving short-term, medium term and long term credit through U.P. state Co-operative and Village Development Banks of which branches exist in all the tehsils of the State. The primary co-operative agricultural loan societies have been established in rural areas of the State up-to the 'Nyaya Panchayat' level, so that, the farmers may get more facilities. About 8597 such societies are functioning in the State. As many as 60 district/Central Co-operative Banks have been established to help the primary co-operative societies. There are about 1453 branches of these banks in the state.

Uttar Pradesh Cooperative Bank (apex bank) established in the year 1944. At present-bank has 82 offices including 29 branches and 40 pay offices and 13 regional offices. The main objectives of U.P. Co-operative Bank are to exercise financial discipline of district/Central Co-operative Banks. During 1996-97, a sum of Rs. 440 crore had been marked to distribute as short-term loan by the cooperatives.

Medium-term loan is made available to farmers and landless members through cooperative societies. Mainly for purchase of milch cattle, bullocks, poultry, birds, pigs, goats, agricultural implements, minor irrigation works, Dunlop cart etc. for a period of three to five years. Rs. 34 crore have been distributed in the state as medium term loan during 1996-97.

Long-term loans are made available for long term investment in agriculture such as minor irrigation work, farm machineries, dairy, wind mill etc., U.P. State Co-operative Agriculture and Village Banks are providing long-term loan 287 such Bank branches are functioning.

In fact co-operative movement had played an important role in financing agriculture & rural development through its credit non-credit societies in India specially southern part. Where people have participated in the programme delicately, honestly and voluntary. The cooperative movement in U.P. also played vital role in financing and increasing production & productivity of agriculture as well as creating additional income and employment of its members. In U.P. there are nine (9) agroclimatic zone and distt. Hamirpur falls under Budel Khand Zone. The annual rainfall in the district is 867.40 mm. It is a dry land area. The economic condition of the farmers are poor. Therefore, for successful cultivation the co-operative credit is instrumental and farmers became able to get better production.

Keeping in view, the present study is undertaken in Distt. Hamirpur with the main objectives:

i) to assess the progress of co-operative development in State, and

ii) to study the role of co-operative in financing agriculture in Distt.

Hamirpur and its impact on agricultural development.

The main crop of the district are Jawar + Arhar, Wheat + Gram, Wheat (HYV) Barley in cereals, Gram, Lentil, Pea, Urd in pulses, Groundut, Linseed, Lahi, Till, Soyabean in Oilseed for which short term & medium term loan are required. Long term loan are required to purchase the heavy machines such as tractor trolly, electric tubewell, etc.

METHODOLOGY

Three stages stratified random sampling technique was used to select the block, villages and farmers.Primary & Secondary data will be collected & comprised for interpretation. Distt. Hamirpur (U.P.) was selected purposively for this study. All the 7 blocks of the district were arranged in descending order of the magnitude of the loan advanced to the farmers. Out of seven block one block namely 'Gohand' having highest loaning was selected. A list of all the villages financed by the co-operative institutions was prepared and arranged in descending order of borrowings. The first five villages viz. Gohand, Jarakhar, Sarsai, Dhanauri and Aunta were selected for the study. A list of all the farmers of selected villages was prepared and classified broadly into two categories i.e. borrowers and non-borrowers. Further borrowers and non-borrowers were stratified into four categories viz. marginal (below 1.00 ha.), small (1.00-2.00ha.), medium (2.00-3.00 ha.) and large (above 3.00 ha.). 100 farms (50 from burrowers and 50 and 50 from non-borrowers) were selected and considered convenient as well as feasible for the study. The numbers of sampled farm was kept in proportionate to their number in each size group for the both groups (i.e. burrowers and non-borrowers).

Result & Discussion

1) Progress of Cooperative in U.P

Since 1950-51, the progress of PACS are given in Table 4.1.

Table 4.1, indicates that in U.P. membership, share capital, deposits, working capital and the loan amount were increased over a time (1950-51—1993-94) but the number of PACS reduced from 26.390 (in 1950-51) to 8597 (in 1993-94).

2) Farm Credit in U.P.

Credit need and its availability from different sources in the State is given in Table 4.2.

Table 4.1 : Progress of PACs in Uttar Pradesh

(Amt. in Crore)

Year	No. of Societies	Membership (in thousand)	Share Capital	Deposits	Working Capital	Loans advanced during			Total Recovery Amount	Recovery %age
						S.T.	M.T.	Total		
1950–51	26390	850	1.00	0.21	3.85	2.28	---	2.28	2.04	---
1960–61	55131	3340	8.89	1.21	34.19	30.98	---	30.98	27.09	92.00
1970–71	23922	5527	21.93	5.04	124.91	48.36	2.98	51.34	46.31	58.88
1980–81	8597	8690	66.68	15.05	466.84	162.61	26.33	188.94	161.96	52.90
1990–91*	8597	12140	126.94	53.61	858.90	353.50	26.49	379.99	468.16	66.38
1993–93*	8597	14857	171.94	64.48	1143.58	737.72	26.77	764.49	N.A.	N.A.

Note : 1. Year 1950–51 to 1988–89 data relates to 30 June 2. Year 1989–90 to 1993–94 data relates to 31st March

* : Provisional

Source : Important Statistics of Uttar Pradesh Cooperative Movement, 1994.

Issued by : Commissioner/Registrar, Cooperative Societies, U.P., Lucknow.

Table 4.2 : Credit Need and Availability

Year	*Average Scale finance (Rs./ha.)*	*Potential Credit need (Rs. Crore)*	*Realistic Credit need (Rs. Crore)*	*Co-op. Credit (Rs. Crore)*	*Comm. Bank (Rs. Crore)*	*Total (Rs. Crore)*	*Credit Gap (Rs. Crore)*
1991–92	1734.00	4397.54	2198.77	669.00	180.00	849.00	1349.58
1992–93	1850.00	4692.72	2346.36	786.00	246.00	1032.00	1314.36
1993–94	1967.00	5011.91	2550.95	950.00	357.00	1307.00	1243.95

Source : Study conducted by ICCMRT.

As per State Census 1991, there are 200.74 lakhs farm holdings in U.P. out of which 893% (179.37 lakhs) belong to small & Marginal farmers. Approximately 51.60% of marginal farmers 45.6% small farmers and 6.10% large farmers are availing institutional credit facilities for short term. On an average a farm needs about Rs. 2000/- on per ha. for various inputs (1994-95 Price level). It is clear from table that co-operative has distributed more credit as compared to commercial banks. During 1994-95, an amount of Rs. 1045.82 crores was made available to the farmers as crop loan and the share of Cooperative Commercial Bank was Rs. 725.32 and 320.50 crores respectively.

3) Productivity of Crop in Uttar Pradesh

Year-wise productivity of crops is given in Table 4.3.

Table 4.3, indicates that per hectare yield was increased in case of Rice, Jawar, Bajara, Maize, Pulses, Wheat, Barley, Gram. But the yield of pea was decreased from 13.95 q/ha (in 1990-91) to 11.16 q/ha in 1994-95. The yield of Arhar was also decreased. This was mainly because of technical gap.

4) Farm Structure of the Sample Farm

Number of farms (borrowers and non-borrowers) cultivated area and average size of farm is given in Table 4.4.

Table 4.4, indicates that the average size of borrower was 2.17 ha. while non-borrowers, it was 1.92 ha. 82.49 percent borrowers farm and 73.59 per cent non-borrowers farms were irriagated.

5) Cropping Patten

Distribution of total cropped area under different crops on the marginal, small, medium and large farms is given in Table 4.5.

Table 4.3 : Productivity of Crops

Qnt./ha.

Sr. No.	Name of Crops	Year 1980–81	1990–91	1994–95
1.	Food Grain			
	a) Rice	10.53	18.27	18.59
	b) Jowar	5.99	9.36	9.06
	c) Bajara	7.37	11.15	10.53
	d) Maize	7.31	13.19	13.31
	e) Kharif Pulses	3.29	3.77	4.30
	f) Wheat	16.50	21.71	25.05
	g) Barley	13.25	17.72	20.57
	h) Gram	8.61	8.79	9.35
	i) Pea	9.49	13.95	11.16
	j) Arhar	14.48	12.34	10.76
	k) Lentil	5.69	7.97	7.78
2.	Oilseeds	5.27	8.45	8.35
3.	Pulses	8.84	9.12	8.87
4.	Cotton	1.27	1.79	1.89
5.	Jute	14.63	15.59	7.39

Table 4.5, indicates that the area under high yielding varieties of wheat and pea was higher on borrowers farms.

As regards different size groups, the area under wheat and pea showed an increasing trend on both the categories of the farms.

6) Cropping Intensity

Cropping intensity is indicator of utilizing land area in a year. The details are given in Table 4.6.

Table 4.6, portrays that cropping intensity was higher on borrowers farm (139.08%) as compared to non-borrowers (129.23%). The intensity of cropping shows decreasing trend with the increase in the size of farms and decreased from 147.97 percent to 132.10 per cent on borrower's farms and 142.18 per cent to 120.11 per cent on non-borrowers farms.

7) Level of Agril. Financing

Co-operatives, Commercial Banks, RRBs & others organisations

Table 4.4 : Number of Farms (Borrowers & Non-borrowers) Cultivated Area and Average Size of Farm

Size Group	No. of Farms		Total Cultivated Area (ha.)		Average Size of holdings (ha.)		Total Irrigated Area (ha.)	
	Borrower	Non-Borrower	Borrower	Non-Borrower	Borrower	Non-Borrower	Borrower	Non-Borrower
Marginal	13	13	9.36 (8.64)	8.06 (8.41)	0.72	0.62	7.15 (76.39)	5.50 (68.24)
Small	15	15	27.00 (24.92)	21.75 (22.70)	1.80	1.45	21.59 (79.96)	15.74 (72.37)
Medium	12	12	33.00 (30.45)	30.00 (31.31)	2.75	2.50	28.93 (87.67)	24.18 (80.60)
Large	10	10	39.00 (35.99)	36.00 (37.58)	3.90	3.60	32.80 (84.10)	28.16 (78.22)
Total	50	50	108.36 (100.00)	95.81 (100.00)	2.17	1.92	90.47 (83.49)	73.58 (76.80)

Note : Figures in parenthesis shows the percentage.

Table 4.5 : Distribution of Total Cropped Area Under Different Crops

Crops	*Size Group*				*Total*
	Marginal	*Small*	*Medium*	*Large*	*Average*
Borrower Farms					
Jowar+Arhar	2.50	6.75	9.42	10.26	28.93
Moong	1.30	4.40	4.90	4.15	14.75
Urd	1.55	3.90	3.50	3.20	12.15
Soybean	1.64	3.82	4.82	5.17	15.45
Wheat	2.53	6.45	9.47	10.88	29.33
Pea	1.50	4.93	5.88	6.60	18.91
Gram	0.90	2.63	3.20	4.05	10.78
Lentil	0.82	2.34	2.03	3.10	8.29
Mustard	0.76	2.15	1.06	2.21	6.18
Others	0.35	1.75	1.94	1.90	5.94
Total	13.85	39.12	46.22	51.52	150.71
Non-Borrower Farms					
Jowar+Arhar	1.96	5.25	8.80	9.45	25.46
Moong	1.05	2.96	2.80	2.30	9.11
Urd	0.92	2.26	3.00	2.10	8.28
Soybean	1.43	2.83	3.52	2.84	10.62
Wheat	2.28	5.90	9.10	9.90	27.18
Pea	1.15	3.19	4.62	5.80	14.76
Gram	0.80	2.38	2.98	4.14	10.30
Lentil	0.71	2.00	1.80	3.08	7.59
Mustard	0.65	1.75	1.35	2.25	6.00
Others	0.51	1.28	1.35	1.38	4.52
Total	11.46	29.80	39.32	43.24	123.82

Table 4.6 : Cropping Intensity of Borrower and Non-Borrower Farms

Size Group	Total cultivated Area (ha.)		Total Cropped Area (ha.)		Cropping Intensity in %age	
	Borrower	Non-Borrower	Borrower	Non-Borrower	Borrower	Non-Borrower
Marginal	9.36	8.06	13.85	11.46	147.97	142.18
Small	27.00	21.75	39.12	29.80	144.89	137.01
Medium	33.00	30.00	46.22	39.32	140.06	131.07
Large	39.00	36.00	51.52	43.24	132.10	120.11
Total	108.36	95.81	150.71	123.82	139.08	129.23

are providing agricultural finance to the sample borrowers. The extent of loan from various institutions are given in Table 4.7.

Table 4.7 : Source-wise Borrowing

(Amt. in Rupees)

Source of Borrowing	Size Group				
	Marginal	Small	Medium	Large	Overall
1. Co-operative Societies	17615.02 (57.83)	51193.88 (60.43)	84614.02 (74.46)	98495.48 (64.80)	251918.40 (66.16)
2. Commercial Banks	4888.83 (16.05)	13249.58 (15.64)	29020.27 (25.54)	53497.16 (35.20)	100655.84 (26.43)
3. Regional Rural Banks	7956.15 (26.12)	20272.54 (23.93)	---	---	28228.69 (7.41)
Others	---	---	---	---	---
Total	30460.00 (100.00)	84716.00 (100.00)	113634.29 (100.00)	151992.64 (100.00)	380802.93 (100.00)

Note : Figures in parenthesis show percentage to total.

Table 4.7, indicates that a some of Rs. 380802.93 was advanced to the sample borrowers by various agencies out of which 66.16 per cent share was from Co-operatives followed by Commercial Banks 26.43 percent and RRBs only 7.41 percent.

8) Purpose-wise Distribution of Loan

The details of purpose wise loan are given in Table 4.8.

Table 4.8 : Purpose-wise Loan of the Sample Borrowers

Activity Borrowing	Amounts (Rs.)				
	Marginal	Small	Medium	Large	Total
A) Agricultural & Allied Sector	17615.02 (57.83)	51193.88 (60.43)	84614.02 (74.46)	98495.48 (64.80)	251918.40 (66.16)
1. Crop Loan	12954.64 (42.53)	40595.91 (47.92)	52103.19 (45.85)	58901.29 (38.75)	164555.03 (43.22)
2. Milch Cattle	4660.38 (15.30)	10597.97 (12.51)	12727.15 (11.20)	12615.43 (8.30)	40600.93 (10.66)
3. Minor Irrigation & Agril. Implement	---	---	19783.68 (17.41)	26978.76 (17.75)	46762.44 (12.28)
B) Non-Agril. Sector	12844.98 (42.17)	33522.12 (39.57)	29020.27 (25.54)	53497.16 (35.20)	128884.53 (33.84)
1. Retail Shop	9713.69 (31.89)	18857.78 (22.26)	---	---	28571.47 (7.50)
2. Village & Cottage Industry	---	8624.09 (10.18)	19997.58 (17.60)	32750.49 (21.55)	61372.16 (16.12)
3. Transport & other Services	3131.29 (10.28)	6040.25 (7.13)	9022.69 (7.94)	20746.67 (13.65)	38940.90 (10.22)
Grand Total	30460.00 (100.00)	84716.00 (100.00)	113634.29 (100.00)	151992.64 (100.00)	380802.93 (100.00)

Note : Figures in parenthesis indicate percentage.

Table 4.8, indicates that various financing institutions were financed sample borrowers for crop loan, milch cattle, & minor irrigation purposes in agriculture sector and for retail shop village & Cottage Industries and transport & other service in non-agricultural sector.

9) Cost of Borrowing

Cost of borrowing is given in Table 4.9.

Table 4.9, indicates that cost of credit was higher or marginal farms (Rs. 21.76 per Rs. 100.00) followed by small Rs. 19.08, medium Rs. 18.00) and Rs. 16.62 on large farms. It was mainly because of the reason that the large farmers were well aware about the procedure and are having good security of loan.

10) Requirement of Loan

Short term, Medium Term, & Land Term Credit requirement was worked out for all categories of the farms. The details are given in Table 4.10.

Table 4.9 : Cost of Credit of the Sample Borrowers

(In Rupees)

Items	*Category of Farmers*			
	Marginal	*Small*	*Medium*	*Large*
1. Interest of Loan	2905.70 (64.35)	8461.88 (73.35)	11208.82 (77.46)	15304.52 (84.23)
2. Loadging, boarding & Travelling	470.00 (10.41)	860.00 (7.45)	885.00 (6.12)	770.00 (4.24)
3. Market fee & Commission	220.00 (4.87)	392.00 (3.40)	375.00 (2.59)	286.00 (1.57)
4. Insurance Premium, Health Certificate etc.	700.00 (15.50)	1400.00 (12.14)	1570.00 910.85)	1420.00 (7.81)
5. No Dues Certificate	100.00 (2.21)	182.00 (1.58)	150.00 (1.04)	110.00 (0.61)
6. Khasra & Khatoni	70.00 (1.55)	140.00 (1.21)	150.00 (1.04)	130.00 (0.71)
7. Others	50.00 (1.11)	100.00 (0.87)	130.00 (0.90)	150.00 (0.83)
Total	4515.70 (100.00)	11535.88 (100.00)	14468.82 (100.00)	18170.52 (100.00)
Amt. incurred/100 Rupee of loan	21.76	19.08	18.07	16.62

Note : Figures in parenthesis is percentage to total.

Table 4.10 : Requirement of Cooperative Credit and its Availability and Utilization on Different Size-group of Farms

Size Group	*Required* (*Rs.*)	*Available Amount* (*Rs.*)	*Utilization of Loan* (*Rs.*)
Marginal	20575.00	17615.00	17615.00
Small	60484.00	51193.88	51193.88
Medium	97610.00	84614.02	84614.02
Large	120342.00	98495.48	98495.48
Total	299011.00	251918.40 (84.25)*	251918.40 (100.00)**

* Shows percentage to required amount.

** Shows percentage to available amount.

Table 4.10, indicates that a sum of Rs. 299011.00 were required by the sampled farmers while only Rs. 251918.40 was made available from the financing institutions. 100 per cent loan amount was observed utilized in the study area.

11) Repayment Performance

The details of repayment is given in Table 4.11.

Table 4.11 : Repayment in Relation to Size of Farms

Size Group	Average size of holding (ha.)	Loan Amount (Rs.)	Repayment (Rs.)		
			Total	Per Farm	Per ha.
Marginal	0.72	17615.02 (100.00)	9179.81 (52.11)	706.14	980.75
Small	1.80	51193.88 (100.00)	28215.63 (55.12)	1881.04	1045.02
Medium	2.75	84614.02 (100.00)	39122.45 (46.24)	3260.20	1185.53
Large	3.90	98495.48 (100.00)	35758.37 (36.30)	3575.84	916.88
Total	2.17	251918.40 (100.00)	112276.26 (44.57)	2245.52	1036.14

Table 4.11, indicates that on an average 44.57 percent of the loan amount was repaid by the borrowers which varied from 36.30 percent on large farms to 55.12 per cent on small farms.

12) Level of Investment, Income & Employment

Employment, Income & Investment level is given in Table 4.12.

Table 4.12, indicates that on an average the employment days come to 335 and income Rs. 7940.37 per farm.

13) (a) Wilful and Non-wilful Defaulters

Table 4.13(A) indicates that the total number of borrowers farms was 50. Out of 50 borrower farms 20 farms were found willful defaulter and 10 farms were non-willful defaulters. The average borrowing of sample farms was Rs. 5038.37.

13) (b) Reason for Non-Repayment

Number of the factors are observed for non-repayment & wilful defaulters. The details are given in Table 4.13(B).

Table 4.12 : Per Farm Level of Investment, Employment and Income

Investment Group	*No. of Farms*	*Cultivated Area (ha.)*	*Income/ Farm (Rs.)*	*Employ-ment farm (days)*
Below—10,000	20.00 (40.00)	20.80 (19.19)	3063.45	175.72
10,000—20,000	13.00 (26.00)	28.55 (26.35)	7280.22	345.28
20,000—30,000	10.00 (20.00)	30.12 (27.80)	10215.95	455.60
30,000—above	7.00 (14.00)	28.89 (26.66)	19849.63	598.85
Total	50.00 (100.00)	108.36 (100.00)	7940.37*	335.02*

Note : Figures in parenthesis shows percentage to total.

* Shows overall average.

Table 4.13(A) : Number of Wilful and Non-wilful Defaulters

Category	*No. of Borrowers*	*No. of Defaulters*		*Average Borrowing (Rs.)*
		Wilful	*Non-wilful*	
Marginal	13	3	4	1355.00
Small	15	5	3	3412.92
Medium	12	6	2	7051.17
Large	10	6	1	9849.55
Total	50	20	10	5038.37

Table 4.13(B), indicates the operational size of land holding, proportion to cash crops to total cropped area, family consumption expenditure, gross income from agriculture, initial amount of loan borrowed, proportion to educated members, proportion of working members to total members, proportion of politically motivated members and average amount of loan overdue are main factor for willful defaulter and non-willful defaulter. The mean value and the differences are indicating that the majority of the defaulters were govern by these factors, up to greater extent as compared to non-willful defaulters.

Thus, it may be concluded that the Co-operative are playing an important role in Agricultural Development.

Table 4.13(B) : Socio-economic Characteristics of wilful and Non-wilful Defaulters

Sr. No.	Socio-economic Characteristics of defaulter	Means		Diffe-erence
		Wilful	Non-wilful	
1.	Operational size of holding (in ha.)	45.40	19.70	25.70
2.	Proportion to cash crops to total cropped area	42.35	24.60	17.75
3.	Family consumption expenditure (in Rs.)	12689.59	8455.38	4234.21
4.	Gross income from Agriculture (in Rs.)	63654.25	28542.63	35111.62
5.	Initial amount of loan borrowed (in Rs.)	7980.46	5189.18	2791.28
6.	Proportion to educated members	80.16	58.63	21.53
7.	Proportion of working members to total members	26.30	42.55	16.25
8.	Proportion of politically influenced member to total members	59.82	24.60	35.22
9.	Average amount of loan overdue (in Rs.)	8671.38	5781.95	2889.43

5

Strategies to Increase Flow of Agricultural Credit through Co-operatives in Orissa

*Dr. B. Patro**

*Dr. (Mrs.) S.R. Das***

*Miss Preyasi Nayak****

Creation of institutional agencies to carefully monitor the flow of capital is one of the responsibilities of a government in an economy. In a developing economy the role of the government is to create 'infrastructure' or 'socio-economic overhead capital' which will sustain not a single production line but a set of great complex economic activities (DATTA, 1973). Economic success in these countries requires transformation in the outlook of the institutions to embrace corporate ideologies and establishment of sophisticated labour and capital market. The job of a credit institution in such an economy is to mobilise corporate and household savings carried out by large number of depositors and channelise them to a capacitively small number of borrowers for different productive purposes (Cairncross, 1962). Investment and capital formation, unlike consumption, is use of resources with an expectation to derive steam of future flow of income. While individuals value present consumption more highly than an equal amount of future consumption, the long-term objective of an economy is to built up a stock of capital with an expectation to ensure flow of

* Reader in Economics, Berhampur University, Berhampur—760 007, Orissa.

** Lecturer in Economics, Berhampur University, Berhampur—760 007, Orissa.

***Research Scholar, Department of Economics, Berhampur University, Berhampur—760 007, Orissa.

income continuously. The perspective under-estimation of the future for an individual is due to his keenness of the immediate present (Ramsey, 1928). In underdeveloped countries this attitude of individuals results in low level of capital. In such economies many economic activities were carried out with little or no capital as compared to similar activities in their developed counterparts (Bauer & Yamey, 1957; Myrdal, 1968). The agricultural sector in such economies has to remain satisfied with traditional, labour-intensive and non-mechanical type of farming.

The planning process in the country has made an effort to channelise adequate capital to the agricultural sector with an objective to generate productive employment. The co-operative credit institutions were given the responsibility of organizing and financing rural economic development since the First Five Year Plan, (GOI, 1952). The co-operatives had been not associations of profiteering but function for mutual service in a democratic manner. The Second Five Year Plan emphasised on linking credit and non-credit agricultural co-operative societies and also divided the agricultural credit organisations into those concerned with short and medium - term finance and those concerned with long-term finance (GOI, 1956). The purpose of the co-operative sector had been to evolve a system of co-operative community organisation touching all aspects of rural life. The subsequent Five Year Plans continue their emphasis on developing the co-operative structure and consolidating their position in the rural economy. The co-operative sector has faced stiff challenges from their competitors since 1969, when it was decided to permit commercial banks to operate in the field of agricultural credit. Inspite of competition of co-operative credit system has withstood the challenge and made significant progress over the years. (All India Agricultural Credit Review Committee Report, 1990).

The New Economic Policy in 1991 made significant changes in the economic administration process of the country. It aimed at macro economic stabilization and restoration (Nair, 1994) of the growth momentum of the economy. The economy has switched over to a free-market system from a regulated-market system. There were a series of structural adjustment programmes to revitalize the deficiency of the economic system. In the national level this scenario has influenced the functioning of the co-operative sector. The total silence of the Financial Sector Reform Committee (M. Narsinmahamam, 1991) on the role of co-operative sector put a big question mark on the future role of the co-operative in India. The logic of the Narsinmhamam Committee, that competitive efficiency and profitability of the financial sector are ownership neutral, is highly debatable. The Eighth Plan Strategy for co-operative credit were to build up co-operative movement as a self-regulated and self-reliant institutional set up by giving autonomy to the co-operative sector. It must involve itself in improving the productivity of the economy and create employment opportunities for the people living in the rural areas. Professionalization of the co-operative sector is another dimension which is to be taken up the priority (GOI, 1992-97).

Co-operative Credit in Orissa

The co-operative structure in Orissa had made a humble beginning in 1904 and at the beginning of First Five Year Plan there were 5145 co-operative societies with a membership of Rs. 2.95 lakhs and working capital of Rs. 4.28 crores. By the end of 1994-95 it has reached to 5878 societies with 53.78 lakhs of membership and a working capital of Rs. 2228.34 crores (R.C.S,.GOO, 1994-95). In Orrisa the co-operative sector was playing a leading role at the time of bank nationalisation. It was supplying 99% of the credit requirement of the rural sector a that time. With the adoption of multi-agency approach the commercial banks and the Regional Rural Banks (RRBs) enter into the picture and in 1979 could able to snatch away 60% of the market share. By 1996 the share of co-operative sector in the rural credit was reduced to an abysmally low figure of 10.2% as against 89.8% of the Commercial banks and RRBs. Table 5.1 below testifies the credit deployment carried out by various rural credit institutions in Orissa.

Table 5.1 : Flow of Rural Credit in Orissa

(Rs. in Crores)

Year	*Co-operatives*	*Commercial Banks*	*Regional Rural Banks*	*Grand Total*
1	2	3	4	5
1986–87	49.00	56.00	19.00	124.0
1987–88	67.90	446.60	162.59	677.1
1988–89	64.50	544.29	197.11	745.6
1989–90	19.70	651.76	226.30	897.7
1990–91	35.07	670.07	209.02	914.2
1991–92	41.06	748.58	198.70	988.3
1992–93	66.43	828.96	219.66	1115.0
1993–94	92.87	889.89	238.29	1221.0
1994–95	122.86	1018.71	282.43	1424.0
1995–96	167.30	1135.10	325.31	1627.7

Sources : Statistical Outline of Orissa, 1988, 1993, 1997.
Economic Suvey of Orissa, 1997–98.

A three tier co-operative credit system exists in Orissa to meet the Short-Term (ST) and Medium-Term (MT) credit in agriculture. The Orissa State Co-operative Banks (OSCB) functions at the apex level, 17 Central Co-operative Banks operate at the intermediate level, 2578 Primary Agricultural Credit Societies (PACS) and 223 Large-sized Adivasi-Multi Purpose Societies (LAMPS) and 6 Farmers Service Societies (FSS) affiliated to Central Co-operative Banks (CCBs) functions at the grass root level, 78% of the members belong to weaker sections and 42% belongs to SCs and STs. The performance of PACS, CCBs and OSCB are presented in Table 5.2.

There is two teir structure to meet the long-term credit in agriculture. The Orissa State Co-operative Agricultural Rural Development Banks (OSCARD) operates at the state level and the Co-operative Agriculture Rural Development Banks (CARD) operates at the base level. There are 57 CARD banks extending long-term credit to 6,000 borrowers amounting 14 crores for the purpose of undertaking land development programmes and modernisation of agricultural operations. The performance of OSCARD and CARD banks are also given in Table 5.2.

The financial sector reform process initiated at the national level to make the system efficiency oriented has two important implications for the future of co-operative credit. One is the involvement of the Commercial banks and RRBs with more advanced technological operations in the rural sector putting the co-operative sector with stiff challenges. The other is concentration of Commercial bank and RRB operations in the urban areas leaving the rural sector to the co-operative system. The Post economic scenario of scheduled Commercial Banks in financing agriculture in Orissa reveals that it has declined from 75% in 1992 to 69% in 1996 (Table 5.1). This means increasing market share for the co-operative sector at the state level. One of the interesting observation is the stagnating share of RRBs in rural credit. RRBs being the main competitor of co-operative sector, this means a favourable environment for the later.

Rural Credit & Agricultural Production in Orissa

In an effort to understand the relationship between rural credit and agricultural production in Orissa we have constructed a multiple regression model. The model specification is

Table 5.2 : Performance of Co-operative Credit Institutions in Orissa

(Rs. in Crores)

Institutions	*Particulars*	*1st* plan 1955–56	*2nd* plan 1960–61	*3rd* plan 1965–66	*4th* plan 1973–74	*5th* plan 1978–79	*6th* plan 1984–85	*7th* plan 1989–90	*Annual* plan 1991–92	*8th* plan 1994–95
ST & MT (PACs, CCBs, OSCBs)	Members (in '000')	495.1	970.8	1227.0	629.1	2205.0	2833.1	3250.4	3304.9	3432.3
	Deposits	2.3	4.5	10.1	20.2	53.8	99.6	146.0	229.7	457.8
	Working Capital	7.7	18.2	41.2	99.8	251.3	489.8	933.7	1055.1	1306.0
	Loans :									
	Advance	4.84	10.1	27.4	29.8	136.6	254.7	128.8	191.5	430.4
	Overdue	0.01	2.4	6.3	32.5	40.0	142.2	327.2	226.4	1114.9
	Profit	0.06	0.5	1.07	1.6	3.0	2.9	2.4	4.4	2.6
Long-Term (OSCARD, CARD	Members (in '000')	0.009	2.026	67.056	267.05	411.05	618.05	705.05	742.05	825.05
	Deposits	---	0.0002	0.07	0.2	0.6	1.3	2.5	3.1	4.8
	Working Capital	0.26	0.3	6.0	47.7	97.3	181.5	215.0	201.6	253.4
	Loans :									
	Advance	0.06	0.16	2.37	6.1	16.1	15.4	1.23	12.5	28.05
	Overdue	---	---	0.02	2.8	4.6	5.7	15.4	15.9	19.7
	Profit	0.0003	0.01	0.03	0.2	0.2	0.2	0.7	0.3	0.2

Sources : Co-operative Movement in India, A Profile 1994–95, Registrar of Co-operative Societies, Orissa.

$$Y - b_0 + b_1 X_1 + b_2 X_2 + b_3 X_3 + u.$$

where, Y = represents the total agricultural production
X_1 = the use of fertilizer
X_2 = area under irrigation
X_3 = rural credit

The regression equation is estimated for the two periods, 1986–92 and 1992–97. This is done with a view to understand the differential role played by the rural credit in the pre-reform and post-reform period.

Table 5.3 : Factors Affecting Agricultural Production in Orissa

Year	Total Agricultural Production (in lakh MT)	Fertilizer used (kgs./ Hect.)	Area under Irrigation (in '000 Hect.)	Rural credit (in crores)
1986–87	54.1	16.37	1788.25	124.0
1987–88	44.5	16.68	1817.17	677.1
1988–89	59.6	22.02	1878.19	745.6
1989–90	66.9	21.7	1977.98	897.7
1990–91	60.3	20.1	2027.37	914.2
1991–92	75.1	20.0	2078.13	988.3
1992–93	62.1	21.6	2120.07	1115.0
1993–94	74.9	21.95	2163.38	1221.0
1994–95	71.4	22.7	2215.61	1424.0
1995–96	70.2	24.6	2273.8	1627.7
1996–97	49.2	30.52	2336.38	1373.0

Source : Economic Survey, Govt. of Orissa, 1996–97.
Statistical Outline of Orissa, 1988, 1993, 1997.

Some of the important observations from the statistical model are:

(i) The fertiliser use and are under irrigation are positively related to agricultural production in the pre-economic reform period whereas rural credit and agricultural production reveals an inverse relationship.

(ii) In the post-economic reform period with fertiliser use and rural credit are negatively related with agricultural production. Only area under irrigation is positively related to agricultural production in the second period.

Table 5.4 : Results of the Multiple Regression Analysis

Sl. No.	*Items*	*1986–92*	*1992–97*
1.	Regression Coefficient	b_0 = –162.4 b_1 = –1.96 b_2 = 0.10 b_3 = –0.02	b_0 = –521.92 b_1 = –9.81 b_2 = 0.40 b_3 = –0.05
2.	Standard Error of Regression Coef.	SE_h = 1.53 SE_b = 0.04 SE_b = 0.02	SE_h = 5.58 SE_b = 0.32 SE_b = 0.06
3.	Standard Error of Y	5.93	4.95
4.	Value of R squared	0.87	0.94
5.	Calculated 't' value	t_1 = 1.29, t_2 = 2.5, t_3 = –1.17	t_1 = 1.75, t_2 = 1.25, t_3 = 0.83
6.	No. of observation	6	5
7.	Degrees of freedom	2	1
8.	Theoretical 't' value at 5% level of significance	4.303	12.706

Source : Data Compiled from Table 5.3.

(iii) The explanatory power of three independent variables appears to be high with 87% in the first period and 94% in the second period.

(iv) The relationship between independent variables and the dependent variable over time shows that it has improved in case of area under irrigation (from 0.10 in the first to 0.40 in the second period) and deteriorated in case of fertiliser use (+1.968 in first period to –9.81 inthe second period) and rural credit (–0.02 in the first period to –0.05 in the second period).

(v) The standard error test (t-test) gives a startling conclusion. None of the regression coefficients are significant either in the first period or in the second period.

Future Strategies of the Co-operative Sector

Under the circumstances narrated in the preceeding sector, it is required that the co-operative system should make out some aggressive strategies to revive the early 1969 scenario at the earliest. It is suggested that the following areas deserve immediate attention to revive the co-operative sector's past glory.

1) Rate of Interest

The Co-operative sector now charges 16.5% rate of interest as against around 12% by the Commercial banks and RRBs. Rate of interest is the price of using borrowed money for different production and investment purposes. The higher rate of interest is due to the existence of three tier system in Co-operative Credit. The OSCB, the CCBs, and the PACS adds their percentages to the NABARD refinance rate of interest. Many co-operative borrowers switch over the other agencies due to high interest rate. To get out of this it is necessary to reduce the three teir system into a two tier system. It may be PACS at the grass root level and OSCB at the state level or CCB at the district level with PACS as their branches and OSCB at the state level.

2) Integration of Short-term & Long-term Credit

In a recent discussion it is noticed that most of the PACS and LAMPS in Orissa are running in loss. Few of them do not have assets equivalent to their losses.It is estimated that for the viable operation of a PAC/LAMB, a minimum credit business of Rs. 25 lakhs is required. As on 1995-96 only 4% (111) of the total (2817) PACS could able to achieve this target. (Status Report, OSCB. 1998) 46% of the total PACS are operating with a business volume of less than 5 lakhs. To make all the PACS viable it is required to channelise 704 crores of production credit through these institutions. The present quantum of credit flow is only Rs. 147 crores. This means it is completely impossible to make all the societies viable in the near future. Two options are available to ease out of the situation. One is to consolidate the weak PACS by margin them with the strong ones and other is to diversify the business activities. The PACS may be asked to handle long-term credit to the agriculture sector in which there is no grassroots agency.The question of integrating the short-term and long-term grassroot credit institutions has been under examination by the All India Rural Credit Review Committee (1969), Hazari Committee (1976), Committee to Review Arrangements for Institutional Credit for Agriculture and Rural Development (CRAFICARD) (1981), Rajgopal Committee (1985) and The Agriculture Credit Review Committee (1990). Many of these committee's suggested for functional co-ordination with the PACS actng as agents of CARD banks for disbursing long-term loans. The Andhra Pradesh Govt. has started this system very recently. This can be experimented in Orissa on a pilot basis in selected PACS. This is expected to raise the volume of business in the PACS and LAMPS.

3) Streamlining of Administration

Another important measure required to make the co-operative system competitive is to streamline the administrative mechanism. Many borrowers of the co-operative institutions allege that it is difficult for them to get timely and adequate credit for meeting their requirements. The PACS normally does not have the power to sanction the loans and has to forward the application to the nearest CCB branch. Sanction and disbursement of such loans take normally between one to two months which is not there with the Commercial banking sector. This invites measure to delegate powers to the functionaries of PACS to immediately sanction and disburse credit atleast upto a small quantity. Other administrative restructuring like adequate salary to the staff, infrastructure in the society offices and adequate professional training are necessary to boost the morale of grassroot co-operative personnel's.

4) Professionalising the Co-operative System

It has come out in many studies that the co-operative sector is the grazing ground for petty politicians. Corruption emanates from these people for their own interest which ruins the future of the co-operative institutions. This requires handing over the administration of the co-operative system to a set of qualified professionals who has commitment and honesty in discharging their services. Such a group can be created even from the public who has interest in co-operation. The remuneration and incentives to such a cadre of people shall be linked to the performance of the society in which they re supposed to work. Fixation of responsibility in case of loss should be a part of accounting requirement in such a system.

5) Improvement in Credit Delivery System

One of the merits of the traditional moneylender is close supervision on the activities of the client with regard to the borrowed money. This facilitates easy and quick recovery at the time of end of the production process. The co-operative sector's disbursement of loans in kind has resulted in many deficiencies. Particularly, the borrowers are dissatisfied with the quality of the product. In recent days, the Reserve Bank of India has started experimenting cash disbursement replacing the old method. The success of this change requires awareness of the customer about the loan burden and circumstantial pressure of other requirements. To tackle these problems it is necessary to stop the practice of loan waiving on political grounds and extent consumption loans and loans for meeting social functions. This will reduce the diversion of the loan to other purposes.

References

1. A.K. Cairncross (1962) : Factors in Economic Development, George Allen & Unwin Ltd., LONDON.
2. Amlan Datta (1973) : Perspectives of Economic Development, Macmillan India, DELHI.
3. A.Koutsoyiannis (1977): Theory of Econometrics, The Macmillan Press Ltd., NEWYORK.
4. Benjamin Higgins (1996): Economic Development, Problems, Principles, and Policies, Universal Book Stall, New Delhi.
5. Co-operative Movement in Orissa: A Profile 1992-93, 1994-95, Registrar of Co-operative Societies, Orissa, Bhubaneswar.
6. Economic Survey, Govt. of Orissa, 1990-91, 1993-94, 1997-98.
7. Gunnar Myrdal (1968): Asian Drama, An Inquiry into the Poverty of Nations, Penguin Books.
8. P.T. Bauer & B.S.Yamey (1957): The Economics of Under-Developed Countries, James Nisbet & Co. Ltd., Cambridge.
9. Reserve Bank of India, Report of the Agricultural Review Committee, 1990.
10. Stastical Outline of Orissa, 1988, 1993-94, Directorate of Economic & Statistics, Orrisa.

6

A Study on the Trend in Growth of Co-operatives in Tamil Nadu with Special Reference to Primary Agricultural Credit Societies

*A. Puspavalli**

Co-operation emphasis the idea of voluntary association of individuals for the achievement of common good. Therefore the basic principles of co-operatives can be summarised as (1) voluntary association (2) democratic organisation (3) self-help organisation-mutual help (4) common welfare and (5) the spirit of dedication and service with absolute honesty and unquestionable integrity. The idea of co-operatives in India as a means of combating indebtedness and supplying rural credit was first suggested in the report of "Fredrich Nicholson" in 1895. A major development in the field of co-operatives since Independence was the appointment of "Rural" Credit Survey Committee" in 1951 by R.B.I.

There are two separate co-operative societies for the provision of agricultural credit *viz* (1) short and medium term credits and (2) the long term credits needs.The former has 3 tier structure consisting of a State Co-operative Bank at the State level; a central co-operative bank at the district level and Primary Agricultural Credit Societies (PACS) at the village level.

Primary Agricultural Credit Societies are mainly responsible for the agricultural co-operative movement in India. They were established in our country after the enactment of co-operative Societies Act in1904. The movement was basically aimed at institutionalise efforts to relieve

* Agricultural Economics Research Centre, University of Madras, Chennai—600 005.

the farmers from the clutches of the money lenders and burden of debts and promote thrift. Gradually they played a positive role.

Keeping the importance of PACS in providing rural credit, it was decided to conduct a study on the trend in growth of PACS in Tamil Nadu with the following objectives.

Objectives

(1) To study the growth rate of components such as Total number of PACS (TNPACS); Total members (TMS); Total Working Capital (TWS); Member per Society (MPS); and Working Capital per Society (WCPS).

(2) To find the relationship between these components.

Methodology

The relevant Secondary data were collected from the office of the Registrar of Co-operative Societies, Chennai and from NABARD tables. The period considered for analysis is from 1982-83 to 95-96.

Statistical Tools Used

1) To find the compound growth rate (CGR) of the components such as TNPACS: TMS: TWC: MPS and WCPS, the following formula was used i.e. $Y–AB^t$.

   where Y = TNPACS/TMS/TWC/MPS/WCPS

   A and B are constants

   t = time

   The Growth rate r was calculated using $(B–1) \times 100 = r$ and it is presented in percentage.

2) A linear trend of the form $Y = ax + b$ was fitted where

   Y = TNPACS/TWC/TMS/MPS/WCPS

   a, b are constants

   x = time.

3) The correlation coefficient between the components was also worked out.

Co-operatives in Tamil Nadu

As per data received from the office of the Registrar of Co-operative Societies Chennai, as on 31.3.97; 55 different types of co-operatives are functioning in Tamilnadu. There are 11038 number of the Societies. Out of 11038 Co-operatives Societies PACS which topped the societies formed about 40.8 per cent followed by the students stores (27.74 percent)

Primary Agricultural Credit Societies in Tamilnadu

It has been observed that out of all types of Co-operatives the growth of PACS was higher than any other type of co-operatives. The growth of different components like total number of Societies (TNS); total memberships (TMS) Member per Society (MPS); Total working Capital; Working capital per Society are given in Table 6.1.

Table 6.1 : PACS : Total number of societies (TNPACS); Total membership (TMS); Member per society (MPS); Total Working Capital (TWC); Working Capital per Society (WCPS) during 1982–83 to 1995–96

Year	*Total No. of PACS*	*TMS (in lakhs)*	*MPS*	*TWC (in lakhs)*	*WCPS (in lakhs)*
1982–83	4691	54.67	1165	40868.83	8.7122
1983–84	4694	56.18	1197	46236.39	9.8501
1984–85	4664	60.19	1291	45584.72	9.7737
1985–86	4655	58.82	1264	47550.70	10.2159
1986–87	4655	60.13	1292	64500.63	13.8562
1987–88	4655	63.39	1362	70150.94	15.0700
1988–89	4655	71.51	1536	101269.67	21.7550
1989–90	4596	61.96	1348	90638.55	19.7211
1990–91	4589	70.05	1526	113957.90	24.8328
1991–92	4587	74.77	1630	120081.26	26.1786
1992–93	4553	83.85	1842	138951.21	30.5186
1993–94	4582	78.75	1719	185651.02	42.6999
1994–95	4553	81.10	1781	NA	NA
1995–96	4545	83.10	1828	286783.51	63.0987

Total Number of PACS in Tamil Nadu

It has been observed from the above Table that more number of PACS was witnessed during the year 83-84 and it was also noticed that the number of PACS has decreased in the subsequent years and remained constant (4655) from 1985-86 to 1988-89 and then it started decreasing in the subsequent years. The lowest number of PACS was noticed in the year 1995-96.

Another interesting point was that when the PACS was lesser in 1995-96 it recorded 1828 MPS; when the PACS was maximum in 1983-84 the MPS was 1197. Therefore, the growth of MPS was increasing at a faster rate. From this it can be inferred that with the collapse of different societies a good section of members enrolled in the Society. The growth of MPS from 1165 in 1982-83 to 1828 in 95-96 is a good indications of peoples attachment with the movement.

Total Working Capitals

It is also noted that working capital was maximum when the number of PACS are minimum in the year 1995-96. On the contrary working capital was lesser when the number of PACS are maximum in the year 1983-84. When the number of PACS are constant during the years 85-86 to 89-90, working capital was on the increase. This shows that the demand for agricultural credit was increasing which was also the good indicator for the involvement of the people in the movement. The working capital per society was 8.7122 lakhs in 1982–83. In1995-96 it had increased to nearly 8 times i.e. 63.0987 lakhs. This shows that the movement has brought more credit into account.

The compound growth rates of different components have been worked out and presented in the Table 6.2.

Table 6.2 : Compound Growth Rates of Different Components

Sl. No.	*Components*	*Growth Rates in percentages*
1.	Total number of Societies (TNPACS)	–0.26
2.	Total Membership (TMS)	3.49
3.	Members per Society (MPS)	4.51
4.	Working Capital (TWC)	15.28
5.	Working Capital per Society (WCPS)	15.18

From the Table it is understood that the component such as TMS, MPS TWC and WCPS had shown positive growth rates while the negative growth rate for TNPACS was noticed as –0.26 percent.

A trend of different component (Y) over the time periods (x) also fitted and presented in the following table. The trend equation is of the form y = ax + b

when Y = TNPACS/TWC/TMS/MPS/WCPS

a, b are constants

x = time

The relative changes in the trends of different components viz. TNPACS; TMS; MPS; TWC; WCPS can be seen from the Table 6.3.

Table 6.3 : Trend of Different Components Y over the Periods (X)

Sl. No.	*Components*	*Trend*	*Trend Equation*
1.	TNPACS	Linear	–6.0418x + 4619.5714
2.	TMS	Linear	1.1754x + 68.4621
3.	MPS	Linear	27.401x + 1484.357
4.	TWC	Linear	5926.7162x + 88786.816
5.	WCPS	Linear	1.3498x + 15.0688

The relative changes can further be studied with the help of correlation co-efficient between these components. Table 6.4 furnishes the correlation coefficient between the components.

Table 6.4 : Correlation Coefficients between the Components

Components	*TNPACS*	*TMS*	*MPS*	*TWC*	*WCPS*
TNPACS	1				
TMS	0.2058	1			
MPS	0.8089	0.2592	1		
TWC	–0.8412	0.2025	0.9752	1	
WCPS	–0.7823	0.2350	0.9082	0.9475	1

The results confirm that there is a negative correlation between TNPACS and TWC. It is also confirmed that there existed negative correlative between TNPACS and WCPS also. Positive correlation could be seen between TNPACS with TMS and MPS; TMS with MPS, TWC and WCPS; A high positive correlation was observed between MPS with TWC & WCPS and TWC with WCPS.

Conclusion

It can be concluded that the present pace of growth of co-operatives has to be geared upto make it more purposeful people's involvement. The present trend indicates that the movement has a better base in rural areas. In order to educate the people about the benefits of co-operatives the base has to be widened.

7

Role of Co-operatives in Financing Agriculture—A Study

Dr. R. N. Misra

Basically the economy of India is rural in character and is thus considered as an agricultural economy. In India the land represents the chief wealth of the nation. Indian agriculture is still is the primitive form and the agricultural potential of the country is yet to be exploited. About 80 percent of Indian population reside in the villages and agriculture constitutes the primary occupation of about 70 per cent of population of our country. For development of agriculture, the government of India is making all out efforts since 1950's. But, still the growth rate of agricultural output is not impressive. From among the various factors for the growth of agriculture, non-availability of adequate and timely agricultural credit is one of the reasons for low productivity. The need for such credit has become all the more important in the context of new strategy and the introduction of high yielding varieties of crops. For rapid agricultural growth, adequate agricultural credit facilities is highly essential.

In India prior to the Co-operative movement a number of small and marginal farmers suffered very seriously from financial crunch and were exploited by indegenous money lenders.

They raised their hands for credit before landlords, money-lenders commission agents, sahukars, mahajans and others who were purely monopolists in the line of money lending market. They studied the weak moments of the farmers to yield their own benefits at the cost of exploitations of the farmers. The Co-operative Credit Societies took its birth after passing the Co-operative credit societies Act in 1904. The

* Dr. Misra, Faculty Member, Department of Commerce, Science College, Hinjilicut, Orissa.

main aim of the Co-operatives was to provides agricultural credit to needy farmers and to save them from the clutches of the money lenders and others.

As per the fundamental principles of Co-operation, the Co-operative credit is guided by the principles of mutual help having service objectives rather than profit. A Co-operative bank, thus must be essentially co-operative in nature and must deal with credit which satisfied the requirement of the agriculturists. A Co-operative bank promotes economic activity and provides banking facilities to the rural people.The Co-operative banks are associated with persons and not with capital. The main aim of the Co-operative bank is to help agriculturists at the time of their need, and also teach them to repay the same at right dates. Co-operative banks in India are classified into —1) Agricultural, 2) Non-Agricultural. The agricultural banks are only concentrated on financing the farmers for the improvement of their lands. Non-agricultural banks are those banks which are not dealing with agricultural finance, but they deal with other type of financing like, financing industries, construction of houses etc. In the field of agricultural credit, generally there are three types of financing are made. These are—1) Short term loan, 2) Medium term loan, and 3) Long term loan. For the above two types of loans, agricultural credit Co-operative societies and other institutions meet the requirement of the farmers and Co-operative Land Development Banks provide long term credit. Classification of agricultural credit has been done, because of the varied needs of the farmers like seasonal agricultural operations, improvement of semi-permanent nature and permanent land improvement including formation of capital assets. Further this classification is also based on the nature of requirement, period of repayment, nature of the security and type of credits. Short term loans are given to the agriculturists for seasonal agricultural operations issued on personal securities and are repayable within eighteen months. Medium terms loans are advanced for purchase for stock, agricultural machinery etc., which are required by the farmers for medium duration. This type of loan is required for semi-permanent nature and generally repayable within 5 years. For long term agricultural purposes like installation of minor irrigation projects, purpose like installation of minor irrigation projects, purchase of heavy agricultural mechaneries, permanent land improvement, construction of farm houses and other permanent investment, repayble between 5 to 20 years are classified as long term loans.

Objective and Scope of the Study

Due to vast gap in the supply and need of credit in the agricultural sector, the multi-agency approach like Co-operatives, Commercial banks, Regional Rural Banks, Government and Private agencies are initiated to meet the requirement of the farmers. Though various financing agencies are there, but the role of Co-operatives in the line of financing cannot be ignored. As the study being fact finding research and is of empirical in nature, the study is confined to only Ganjam district of Orissa. For this purpose I have taken 100 (One Hundred) agriculturists, from the rural, Semi-urban and Urban areas of the district. For this purpose Random sampling method has been adopted by taking an appropriate questionnaire. Again the study has covered a period of five years from 1991–1992 to 1995–1996 and the financing style of the Co-operatives to farmers of the district towards agriculture is to be taken for the purpose of the study. The primary data are collected as per the informations given by the sample borrowers of the study district. So the informations supplied by them (as per the questionnaire) at the time of survey cannot be taken as hundred per cent accurate.

Essentials of Agricultural Credit

The necessity of credit emanate from a number of vital factors. But credit may not necessarily be taken or be seen as to be a sign of weakness. Nevertheless, borrowing may be abused and indebtedness may be a symptom and a cause of danger. Incurring debt for agricultural, production is not bad. Even in most advanced countries agriculturists taken loans to carry on their work. Such a debt can be repaid out of the income generated from production. But our agriculturists avail debt also for non-productive purposes like family expenditure on consumption, performance of social functions connected with marriage, birth and death ceremonies, legal expenses etc. Since, these loans taken by them contribute very little towards production, it is not possible for them for repayment of loans.

Credit is essential to agriculture for the purpose of increasing its productivity. More than 50 (Fifty) per cent of the population of the rural area live below the poverty line (BPL). To uplift the living standard of these people, greater importance has been given to agriculure. Financial assistance is essential for farmers to increase their agricultural production. Agriculture cannot be developed unless proper credit facilities are made available to the peasantry class in the negelected rural areas of the country. The need for credit has become more important in the context of new strategy and the introduction of high yielding varieties and also mechanised cultivation and for making the agriculture upto date and modern, the basic need is adequate financing. For agricultgural credit, two main factors are to be taken into consideration—(*i*) The purpose of credit (*ii*) The length of period of credit. Purposewise, every farmer needs different types of credit, Viz., development credit, production credit, marketing credit and consumption credit. Development credit is required by the farmers to make investments on the farm land which include—(a) Purchase of land, implements and farm machinery etc., (b) Development of irrigation, construction of tube-well, canals; renovation of old wells, tanks, installations of pump set etc., (c) Reconstruction of land, land levelling, land shaping, laying out field channels, exits etc., (d) Construction of farm structures, cattle shed, silopits, farm fencing, godowns, gobar gas plants etc., (e) Development of horticulture, fruit garden, plantation and nursery etc., and (f) Development of dairy, poultry, piggery, fishery and sericulture etc.

Production credit is required by the farmers to increase their agricultural production. This type of credit is for purchasing seeds, fertilizers, pesticides, payment of wages etc. Credit is also required for the marketing of goods, procurement of goods or recovery of all expenses incurred for harvesting of goods, transportation charges, storing charges etc. Payment of expenses for processing the product, ware-housing charges are usually taken as consumption credit.

The financial requirement of the farmers is also based on the length of credit required. Generally, advances are given in three types viz; Short term, Medium term, and Long term basis. Hiring of labour, purchase of seeds, fertilizers etc., are placed under the short term finance. Repairs of dugwell, tanks, ware-house etc., purchae of live stock, minor irrigation, minor land improvement etc., are treated as intermediate term credit. Long-term credit is mostly used for permanent improvement of land, purchse of land machinery, digging of wells, tanks, construction of farm houses, cattle shed, development of irrigation etc., are generally considered as long term finance.

Supply of Agricultural Credit by Co-operatives

Sources of credit is an important factor which influence the propensity to borrow. Credit supply and its proper use are two important instruments for agricultural growth. The different sources of supplying agricultural credit are Co-operatives, Commercial Banks and Regional Rural Banks under the fold of the institutional sources. But the study is confined to Co-operative Banks. The flow of credit to the borrowers during the period of study i.e., from 1991-92 to 1995-96 from the Co-operatives is illustrated in the Table 7.1.

Table 7.1 : Flow of Credit from the Co-operatives to the Sample Borrowing during the Period from 1991–92 to 1995–96 in the Sample District

Year	*Sample Borrowers*	*Amout (Rs. in '000)*
1991–92	25	09.2
1992–93	22	10.7
1993–94	27	13.5
1994–95	14	25.7
1995–96	12	20.4
Total	100	79.5

Source : Compiled from questionnaire.

Table 7.1 reveals that out of the hundred sample borrowers, they have borrowed Rs. 79.5 thousand during the period of study. In the year 91–92 the number of borrowers are next to highest but flow of fund is lowest. But the flow of fund is highest in the year 1994–95.

Supply of credit according to area is divided into urban, semi-urban, and rural in the same district is illustrated in the Table 7.2.

Table 7.2 : Area-wise Distribution of Credit by the Sample Borrowers during the Period of Study

(Rs. in '000)

Year	*Urban*		*Semi-Urban*		*Rural*		*Total*	
	No. of Borro-wers	Amt.	No. of Borro-wers	Amt	No. of Borro-wers	Amt.	No. of Borro-wer	Amt.
1991–92	02	2.0	07	3.0	16	4.2	25	9.2
1992–93	---	---	10	4.6	12	6.1	22	10.7
1993–94	04	6.5	11	3.2	12	3.8	27	13.5
1994–95	04	9.5	5	9.0	5	7.2	14	25.7
1995–96	05	10.4	3	4.6	4	5.4	12	20.4
	15 (15%)	28.4 (35.5%)	36 (36%)	24.4 (30.8%)	49 (49%)	26.7 (33.7%)	100 (100%)	79.5 (100%)

Note : Figure in brackets indicate percentage.
Source : Compiled from questionnaire.

Table 7.2 reveals that 15 or 15% borrowers of urban areas are taken agricultural loan. But their flow of credit is highest (Rs. 35.5) with comparison to other two areas. Rural borrowers contribute 49% of the total borrowers of the district but the flow of fund is only 33.7%. Here the urban borrowers are clevers and they manage to get more funds from the cooperatives with comparison to rural borrowers. Though the main aim of the Co-operatives to finance the rural agriculturists, but the urban borrowers are able to get more funds by influencing the bank personnel.

Now, the sample borrowers are classified into three categories; scheduled caste, scheduled tribe and general. The flow of credit-caste, wise is illustrated in Table 7.3.

Table 7.3 : Distribution of Credit to the Sample Borrowers According to Caste during the Period of Study

Scheduled Tribe		*Scheduled Caste*		*General*		*Total (Rs. in '000)*	
No. of Borro-wers	*Amt.*	*No. of Borro-wers*	*Amt*	*No. of Borro-wers*	*Amt.*	*No. of Borro-wer*	*Amt.*
17 (17%)	4.0 (5.0 app.)	23 (23%)	8.2 (11.0 app.)	60 (60%)	67.3 (84% app.)	100 (100%)	79.5 (100%)

Note : Figures in brackets under each column indicate percentage.
Source : Compiled from questionnaire.

General caste borrowers of the Ganjam district during the period of study have availed nearly 84% of the funds supplied by the cooperative banks. But the percentage of borrowers are only 60%. Rest 40% borrowers availed only 16% of the loans. As the general borrowers are more literate with comparison to other two borrowers, they could manage to arrange for more loans from the Co-operative banks.

Term-wise supply of agricultural credit of the sample district during the period of study is illustrated in Table 7.4.

Of the total borrowers, 55% of borrowers, borrowed short term loan amounting Rs.32.5 thousand. But the rest of the borrowers borrowed Rs. 47.0 thousand which is higher than short term borrowing. As the short term loans are for short term purpose and loans are of less amount, the short term financing is less than comparison to other two types of loans.

Table 7.4 : Term-wise Supply of Agricultural Credit to the Sample Borrowers of Ganjam District during the Period of Study

Short-Term		*Medium-Term*		*Long-Term*		*Total (Rs. in '000)*	
B	*Amt.*	*B*	*Amt.*	*B*	*Amt.*	*B*	*Amt.*
55 (55)	32.5 (46.2)	33 (33)	25.3 (31.6)	12 (12)	11.7 (22.2)	100 (100)	79.5 (100)

Note : Figures in brackets under each column indicate percentage.
Source : Compiled from questionnaire.
B = Borrower

The Co-operative provide funds to sample borrowers to the district in cash, or in kind or both. Generally cash credit is provided to the loances to meet direct expenses relating to agricultural activities like payment of wages, purchase of fertilisers, seeds etc., machinery, bullocks, and cart etc., are supplied under kind component. But in certain cases both cash and kind loans are also provided to the beneficiaries. The mode of supply of loans during the period of study to the sample borrowers are explained in the Table 7.5.

Table 7.5 : Mode of Borrowing by the Sample Borrowers during the Period of Study

(Rs. in '000)

Only Cash		*Only Kind*		*Cash & Kind*		*Total*	
B	*Amt.*	*B*	*Amt.*	*B*	*Amt.*	*B*	*Amt.*
17 (17)	17.4 (22.6)	32 (32)	28.2 (35.2)	51 (51)	33.9 (42.2)	100 (100)	79.5 (100)

Note : Figures in brackets under each column indicate percentage.
Source : Compiled from questionnaire.
B = Borrower

Due to misuse of cash by the borrowers, loan provided under kind component comes into existence. Supply of credit of cash and kind is most popular and 51(51%) borrowers have been lent Rs. 33.9 thousand on cash & kind, whereas it is Rs. 17.4 thousand for cash component and Rs. 28.2 for kind comonent (Rs. 45.6 thousand for both).

Literacy also plays a vital role in a borrowings. Supply of credit on the basis of literacy and illiteracy is illustrated in the Table 7.6.

Table 7.6 : Supply of Credit to the Sample Borrowers during the Period of Study

(Rs. in '000)

Literate Borrowers		*Illiterate Borrowers*		*Total*	
No.	*Amt.*	*No.*	*Amt.*	*No.*	*Amt.*
63 (63)	52.1 (66 app.)	47 (47)	27.4 (34 app.)	100 (100)	79.5 (100)

Note : Figures in brackets under each column indicate percentage.
Source : Compiled from questionnaire.

Out of the total sample borrowers 63% of the borrowers are literates and the rest 47% are illiterates. But illiterate 47% borrowers have been taken 34% of the loan and rest 66% have been supplied to literate beneficiaries. It seems that the literate borrowers are more conversant about lending procedures than the illiteate ones, which probably made them to avail of more credit.

Loan supplied by co-operatives for agricultural purposes are sufficient to meet the purpose of the borrowers or not, is illustrate in Table 7.7.

Table 7.7 : Sufficiency of Co-operative Loan Supplied by the Sample Borrowers of Ganjam District during the Period of Study

Sufficient to meet the purpose	*Not Sufficient to meet the purpose*	*Total Borrowers*
42	58	100

Source : Compiled from questionnaire.

According to the Table 7.7 outof 100 sample borrowers 58% borrowers are not satisfied by the supply of loan and rest 42% are satisfied with the supply of loan. The loan supplied by the Co-operatives are not sufficient to meet the purpose so they are not satisfied with the supply of credit.

Findings

General caste borrowers are taken lions share in the agriculture credit supplied by the sample borrowers. 60% borrowers are general caste borrowers and they take nearly 84% of the loan and rest 16% are distributed to scheduled tribe and scheduled caste borrowers. Short-term supply of loan plays a vital role in the line of agricultural finance. 55% of borrowers prefer short term finance and 33% on medium-term loan and rest 12% goes to long-term borrowers. Cash and kind component has played a leading role in - agricultural finance of sample borrowers and Rs. 33.9 thousand ahve been supplied to these borrowers. Literate borrowers of the district are able to influence the bank personnel and they have taken greater part of the loan (66%) in comparison to illiterate borrowers.As the loan supplied by Co-operatives to the sample borrowers of the district are not sufficient to meet their purpose, they are not satisfied in the lending procedure, 58% of the sample borrowers are not satisfied with the lending procedure of the Co-operatives.

Suggestions

1. Credit may not be sanctioned according to the approved schemes of the lending institutions alone. It must be supplied according to the need of the borrowers. Bank personnel should visit the borrowers before supply of loan to examine their need.
2. Timely lending, repeated approach and proper supervision by the bank personnel may pursue the borrowers for proper utilistaion and repayment of loan, and it can be taken into consideration.
3. More steps should be taken to supply agricultural loan to the rural borrowers in steed of urban borrowers.
4. Rural lending are provided only of production purposes. As the most of the borrowers are below the living standard; consumption credit may please be supplied to the farmes for proper use of the agricultural loan.
5. An agricultural card must be given to all agricultural farmers. In the card, entire things about the farmer like his land position, loan taken, repayment of loan, tax payment, payment of land tax etc. must be mentioned. Loan should not be sanctioned before examined of agricultural card.
6. Crop Insurance and other Insurance must be made according to the purpose of loan supplied.
7. Application of for loan and other pre-borrowing procedure and sanction of loan must be finished before cultivation, so loan will be supplied to the beneficiaries at an early date and the borrowes can use the loan properly.

8. Loan should not be supplied by organising 'Krishi Mala' for fulfilment of the target of the Govt. Target oriented finance may tempt the borrowers for misuse of loan.
9. Bank personnel should have good relation with the borrowers, their behaviour towards the agriculturists must be good, simple and understandable. They should not be harrased from time to time before it was sanctioned.
10. Steps must be taken by the village workers and bank personnel on pre-lending expenses. If the pre-lending expenses are more, the use of loan will be less.

References

1. Banerjee,P.K. "*Indian Agricultural Economy—Financing Small Farmers*", Chetna Publications, New Delhi.
2. Patnaik, U.C; and Misra R.N; "*Rural Banking in India*", Anmol Publications (P) Ltd. New-Delhi, 1993.
3. Rane, A. A; "*Agricultural Credit in India, Rural India*", Ishwardas Mansions, Bombay, 1980.
4. Misra, R.N.; "Role of Co-operative Banks in Financing Long Term Agricultural Credit"; M.Phill. Dissertation (Commerce)—Awarded by Berhampur University—1983.
5. Desai, S.S.M.; "*Rural Banking in India*", Himalaya Publishing House, Delhi, 1986.
6. Gupta, S.C; "*Development Banking for Rural Development*", Indian Book Centre (P) Ltd. Delhi, 1986.
7. Bedi R.D.; "*Theory, History and Practice of Co-operation*, Loyal Books Depot, Meerut, 1986.

8

Co-operatives Movement in Southern Districts of Tamil Nadu

*Prof. Raghuraman**

This paper deals with co-operatives in Virudunagar Sivaksi and Srivilliputur.

Co-operative Movement in Virdunagar Region

Co-operative movement in this area aim at helping the rural poor and the middle class.

Primary Agricultural Co-operative Banks.

In Virudunagar district there are 185 primary agricultural co-operative banks. They disburse crop loans, non-agricultural, medium term loans, jewel-loan, consumer loan, housing loan, entrepreneur loans etc.

During 1997-98, Rs. 8.96 crores crop loans, Rs. 3.9 crores medium term loans, Rs. 60.13 crores jewel loans. Rs. 24.86 lakhs housing loan etc. have been disbursed.

Rs. 1.36 crores as non-farm credit has also been disbursed.

Deposits

Two primary co-operative agricultural banks have deposits of more than Rs. 5 crores. Twenty primary agricultural co-operative banks have more than one crore as deposits. Fifteen co-operative banks have more than 50 lakhs of deposits.

Two co-operative banks have no defaulters in repayment.

* Prof. Raghuraman Narayan, is the Head of the P.G. Department of Economics, Madurai College (Autonomous), Madurai (Tamil Nadu)—625011

Seventeen co-operative banks have safety lockers.

Long Term Loans

In Virudunagar region 5 Co-op. agricultural banks and Rural Development banks have disbursed Rs. 3.80 crores as long term loans. During the current financial year (1997-98) Rs. 86.87 lakhs has been disbursed as long term loan.

The authority to grant long term loans rests with State Co-operative bank. They have to check the use of credit. Now, the power has been given to Bank Directors.

Co-operative Urban Banks

In Virudunagar district, there are 5 Co-operative urban Banks. All the five command deposits between Rs. 10-15 crores. During the current financial year (97-98) the Urban banks have advanced Jewel loans Rs. 21.5 crores; Non-farm loans Rs. 2.25 crores; Housing loans of Rs. 60 lakhs;

The above five urban co-operative banks run on good profit. They have declared dividend 21%.

Workers Thrift Societies

There are sixty thrift societies for government servants, teachers, other workers Unions. They provide cash credit and consumer loans. During the current year (1997–98) they have advanced Rs. 1254 lakhs as credit. Out of sixty 53 societies are running on profit.

Service Co-operatives

To help the farmers they buy agricultural produce from farmers and sell, it for a good price. During 1997-98 Rs. 1250 lakh worth of agricultural goods are bought and sold.

Co-operation and Education

In Tamilnadu, there are three technical institutes operating. There is one institute in Thiruchuli, conducted by Virudunagar co-operative unions. They provide computer education for 35 people. (1997-98).

Dhalavaipuram Co-operative Health Society

It was started in 18th March 1956 with a capital of Rs. 5000 and to all members of 500.

They provide the following services. Delivery case, intensive care unit, X-ray unit, surgical unit and clinical laboratory.

The hospital treats around 100-150 outdoor patients, 26 indoor patients, five delivery cases. Every month 15 people undergo family planning operations.

Consumers Co-operatives

There are 32 consumer's co-operatives in Virudunagar district. During the current period (97-98) Rs. 3750 lakh consumer goods have been sold.

Co-operative Management Institute

During 1997-98 academic years 500 students were trained in managing co-operatives. There are 10 co-operative management training centres are there in the State of Tamilnadu. The Thyagi Sankaralingnar Management Institute occupies second position in the state.

Leasers Co-operative Farms

In Devadhnam, there is a leasers co-operative farm. There is a tample farm to the extent of 241 acres. It has been leased to members in the co-oepratives. The co-operative collects due in the form of paddy, haystock and give it to the temple.

Co-operative Kerosine Sales Centre

As people do not get the right measurement of kerosine, the kerosine co-operatives provide kerosine to the public.

Table 8.1 : Development of Co-operatives in Virudunagar

	Srivili-putur	*Arupu-kottai*	*Total*
1. Primary Agricultural Co-operatives	98	85	183
2. Co-op. Rural Banks	1	---	1
3. Tillers Co-operatives	1	---	1
4. Agricultural Producers Sales Co-op.	3	2	5
5. Urban Co-op. Banks	4	1	5
6. Distt. Co-op. Printing	---	1	1
7. Central Co-op. Bank	---	1	1
8. Workers' Co-op. Thrift Society	31	29	60
9. Primary Agricultural and Rural Development Bank	2	3	5
10. Wholesale Co-op. Stores	1	1	2

(Contd.)

Table 8.1 : (Contd.)

	Srivili-putur	*Arupu-kottai*	*Total*
11. Rural Co-op. Stores	6	5	11
12. Urban Co-op. Stores	2	2	4
13. Employees Co-op. Stores	13	4	17
14. Students Co-op. Stores	54	36	90
15. Co-op. Union	---	1	1
16. Leasers Co-op. Farm	2	---	2
17. Labour Contract Co-op.	3	1	4
18. Barbers Co-operative	2	---	2
19. Health Co-operative	1	---	1
20. Vegetable Producers' Co-operative	1	---	1
21. Co-operative Training	1	--	1
22. Urban Co-operative Credit Society	--	1	1
	226	173	399

In Virudunagar district, district Consumer's whole sale stores takes consumers goods from Tamilnadu Consumers good Corporation and sell it to fair-price shops. Rajapalayam and Virudunagar whole sale societies sell goods to the fair-price shops at Sathur, Arupukottai, Thiruchozhi, Kariapatti and Sivakasi Taluks. They have 82 fair-price shops in their region.

Fair-Price Shops

Table 8.2 : Fair-price Shops in the Region

Primary Agricultural Co-operative Banks	410
Co-operatives Stores	113
Co-operatives Sales Societies	12
Contract Workers Co-op.	1
Total	536

Women Fair-Price Shops

There are three fair-price shops for women only, run by women from July 1995.

Virudunagar Co-operatives

Present Position

The Bank function in its own buildings in Virudunagar,Watrap, Sathur, Sirivilipurtur.

In Sivaksi it is going to open its 31st branch at Coronation colony.

At Rajapalayam it has constructed a new cotton market at the cost of Rs. 30 lakhs.

At Thiruzhi, it has constructed a branch building at the cost of Rs. 22 lakhs.

Future Plans

Now the co-operatives are under the special scheme of NABARD for it's development from 1994–95 to 98–99. It has crossed it's target of fixed deposits of Rs.140 crores.

Table 8.3 : Future Targets of Virudunagar Co-operatives

a) Share Capital	Rs. 22.83 crores.
b) Allocation	Rs. 15.30 crores.
c) Advances	Rs. 266 crores.

Prospects of Future Advance Policy

(Under guidelines of NABARD)

For small scale units the advances are to be increased from 10 lakhs to 15 lakhs (Rs.)

Loans are to be advanced to specialists like eye, dental surgeons to establish their own practice centres. ENT and Vetenary surgeons are also to be covered.

Loans to be advanced to bulldozers, Earth movers purchases also.

Virudunagar Central Co-operative Bank

It was started in 1993 with 20 branches. Now it has 30 branches (1998).

It has dedicated itself for rural upliftment. They provide financial help for agriculturists and weavers.

Loans are given for the following needs :

1. Loan to micro entrepreneurs in rural area to start industries.
2. To develop transport.

3. Cash-credit for monthly wages earners through promoting thrift societies.
4. Loan to registered Engineers and Doctors to establish their services.
5. Construction of new house, repair the old one-loan upto 5 lakhs.
6. Loans less than Rs. 2000/- for people below the poverty line to improve their income earning.
7. Loans upto 10 lakhs for education, medical expenses for business etc., by taking the house as mortgage.
8. Loans to buy tractors, power tillers etc.
9. Jewel loan upto one lakh.

Table 8.4 : Development of the Central Co-operative

Period 1993–98	*% increase*
Long-term deposits	93 %
Shares	85 %
Running Capital	26 %
Branch Expansion	50 %
Short-term Loans	49 %

Source : Office Reocords of the Central Co-operative Bank.

The co-operatives movement in Virudunagar district is laudable. When the movement shows a downward trend in many parts of the country, it has shown a good growth trend.

Among the various forms of co-operative societies certain categories have shown remarkable growth, Agricultural co-operative societies and students co-operative stores forms a considerable growth areas. Next come Workers' co-operative thrift societies.

The area of co-operation in Virudunagar district has some unique fields of operation. Barbers co-operatives is unique in the State. (Tamilnadu)

Recently, the high price of Onions changed the political scene in the country. It was complained by the Prime Minister, Revered A.B Vajpayee that the reason is only the act of middlemen. In Virudunagar they have formed Vegetable Co-operatives. Spread of such institutions may reduce the price spread in vegetables, thereby both producers and consumers (end) may be benefited.

Leasers co-operative farms is another unique feature. Temple lands are cultivated by the members and the due are given to temple. They may be extended to temple lands of Tamilnadu to protect the temple lands enjoyed by few families. It is pity that temple with lands running into hundreds of fertiled acres of land do not get revenue even to lit the lamp. The Government is spending it's time about the use of languages in temple rituals. Instead they may follow Virudunagar example are spread the benefit of the temple lands to many landless and marginal farmers, thereby save the temples also.

Exclusive women fair-price shops is another unique feature.

Now a days health care has become a more expensive item of expenditure for poor people also. Even a World Bank study reveals that 80% of the poor people go only to private hospitals.

It is unique that Virudunagar district has one Co-operative hospital with Male and female Doctors and beds for inpatients.

Conclusion

The study of co-operative movement in Virudunagar and Tuticorin districts of Southern District of Tamilnadu throws more light regarding the future of the movement and the lines are drawn for future course.

The co-operative movement in Virudunagar districts shows the new lines on which the movement can be planned for further development.

The Unique Feature (Virudunagar)

The area of operation is an agrarian area. Dry lands, Industries (large-medium and small) handloom etc.

The women co-operatives and their success in the field of public distribution shows the future line of development of the movement.

Co-operative institutions draws a middle (educational) line between private and public sector. People even in rural areas do not prefer free Government or Panchayat Union run schools.The poor selection of teachers and lack of commitment drive even a lower middle class persons to choose more expensive private schools. People are prepared to pay money for schooling if it is worthwhile. The co-operatives can enter schooling by selecting teachers on the basis of merit and run it on cost-basis.

We can apply the indicator theory to arrive at results. The mushgroom growth of English medium schools even in villages reveals the preference of the people. And so the self- financing college.

Co-operation may be a success in this field if they do not follow government reservation policy in recruitment of teachers.

Transport is a must for development of an area. Already the co-operative lend money to buy small transport vehicles. They can even run mini busses. In Tuticorin district, the targets are higher and the achievements are low. The Excess funds can be used for this.

Co-operative medical care is a unique feature of Virudunagar co-operatives. It can be followed by other co-operatives in the other part of the country.

Case Studies

The above details present a comprehensive picture of the co-operative movement in Virudunagar district. Now an attempt has been made to highlight particular field of co-operation in which remarkable advancement has been made in this area. The area of study is a long stretch of dry lands. The main occupation in the past was rearing cow and production of milk. But, in the report presented by the Virudunagar district co-operative, no specific mention has been made on milk co-operatives. However, details are available on handloom co-operatives in this area. Other than dairying, vegetable gardens and cotton fields are the main backdrop of the people.

The following figures may justify my selection of the case study.

Total number of handlooms in the district	35000
No. of handlooms brought under the co-op. fold	33000
Active looms	19447
Idle looms	14462

Handloom Concentrated Areas

a) Arupukottai b) Sriviliputur c) Sundrapandiapuram
d) Rajapalayam e) Chatrapatti.

Total number of weavers co-operative societies and their working capital :

Primary co-operative weavers Societies		87
Industrial type of weavers Co-ops.	16	
Powerloom weavers Co-op. Society	1	
Total	104	
Working capital	Rs. 2189 lakhs	

Finances

Share capital and deposits the State Government has already put in Central co-operative bank. NABARD provides cash credit at concessional rate to the co-operatives through Central co-operative bank. During the year 1998-99 it has provided cash-credit to the value of Rs.1981 lakhs.

Table 8.5 : Progress of Virudunagar handloom Co-operatives

(figures in lakhs)

Production	*Metre*	*Value (Rs.)*	*Sales (Rs.)*
1990–91	108	1868	1904
1991–92	116	1934	2003
1992–93	127	1934	2104
1993–94	136	2248	2367
1994–95	148	2338	2772
1995–96	173	2746	3240
1997–98	170	2693	2964

The weavers co-operatives have failed to earn profit only one year—1996-97. During 1995-96 they have earned highest level of profits. In general the scheme is a success.

Marketing of Cloth

They mainly sell their products through Co-optex.The varieties are the following:

Polystar sirting, dhoties, art silk sarees, lungis, etc. They sell them by 20% rebate.

Promotional Schemes

Handloom development centre, quality dyeing centre, project package scheme.

They freely distribute school uniform to school children.

Welfare Scheme for Weavers

The weavers save 4% of their wages and the Government contribute another 4%. Besides, Central Government contribute another 4%.

Family pension scheme is also in operation. Old age pension, housing loans are other welfare measures. Health insurance is extended to workers.

Case Study II

Thiruthangal Co-operative Agricultural Primary Society

I have taken up the case study of this society as it was studied Eighty years ago. There is a reference about this society in a book 'Slater Villages' published by 1914. Probably this was the first primary agricultural society started in the country. Now a study is made after eight plus years.

It was started much ahead of the formation of agricultural department. In the free India it was registered as Co-op. Society in the year 1957 on Nov., 23.

It covers Thiruthangal. East Thiruthangal, Narayananapuram etc.

Total Membership 5584

Table 8.6 : The Details of Thiruthangal Co-operative Agricultural Society

(figures in lakhs)

Share Capital :	
Membership	11.99
Govt.	3.14
Fixed Deposits :	
Permanent Deposits	311.49 (Rs.)
Amudasurabi Deposit	280.00
Current	14.52
Savings Account	114.10
others	0.59
Total	721.01

Unlike other co-operative they do not get loan either from Central Co-operative bank or any other institutions. They disburse loans from their own deposits.

Thrithangal is unique in it's nature that way. They take immediate action on defaulters.

Loans

Short-term farm loan

Medium-term IRDP loan

Non-plan medium-term loans for small business or industry.

Non-farm Loans

Besides they advance money to doctors. Engineers, housing purchase of small transport vehicles, consumer goods, jwel loans.

Advancing educational loans, Marriage loans, construction of Commercial places are it's special features.

They run four fair-price shops covering 1680 cards. No complaint has been made so far.

They have declared highest dividend to the share holders in the district. They have declared 14% dividend.

Table 8.7 : Positionof Profit

Year	*Profits (in Rs. lakhs)*
1995–96	17.26
1996–97	18.76
1997–98	19.57

Thrithangal is an important place for Vaishnavites. Thiruthangal leans - abode of Godess Lakshmi. It is one among the 108 Vaishnavite shrines important for pilgrims.

It is a most ideal Society in the country.

Jwel loans form the major item of advances.

Tuticorin District

A note on Farm co-operatives in Tuticorin district.

It was alleged that the main reason for soaring prices is the part played by middlemen in marketing agricultural produce. The Onion and Potato prices went out of reach for the poor consumers. The solution is the eradication of middle men.

When the outgoing Chairman of Ananand: the Workd's biggest co-operative in Milk said: the main aim of the co-operative is not to earn huge profit, but to give higher prices for the producers'.

Co-operative marketing is a key to the development of agrarian sector.They should go Corporate in marketing. In fact Anand went on the line of success only when they turned to marketing techniques. Vale-added products kept the co-operative on profit lines. From milk (primary) they went to value addition of milk based products, like; powder, ice-cream, cheese, yogart etc. It is a proven case unless marketing is carried out on market needs agricultural produce may not get the desired price for the farmers.

The main aim of co-operatives in the country is to protect and promote the life of farmers.

Now let us turn our views on agricultural marketing in Tuticorin district of Southern Tamilnadu.

In Tuticorin the Agricultural Co-operative Marketing Societies help 2400 farmers by way of purchasing agricultural products and selling them through societies.

The Co-operatives buy cotton, chillies and Coriander and sell them. A target of Rs. 1110 lakhs has been fixed upto 1999 March. As on October 30, 98; Rs. 731 lakhs worth of agricultural produce have been bought and sold helping 2453 farmers.

Out of the 378 co-operatives in the district elections have been completed in 377 societies.There 158 Primacy agricultural co-operatives in the district (Banks); have distributed Rs. 470.76 lakhs short-term crop loan benefiting 2707 beneficiaries.

Under IRDP and THADCO schemes against the target of Rs. 370 lakhs, medium term loans to the tune of Rs. 32.42 lakhs had been issued to 472 beneficiaries during the same period.

In the district there are 12 branches of Central co-op. Banks, 158 Primary Agricultural Credit Banks, 8 co-operative Urban banks and 3 Land Development Banks. They put together, against the target of Rs. 12800 lakhs jwel loans Rs. 66370 lakhs have been issued for1.23 lakh beneficiaries upto 31st October, 1998.

Non-farm Loans

In non-farming against the target of Rs. 525 lakhs, Rs. 365.2 lakhs had been disbursed during the current financial year. (Urban banks)

Central co-operative banks, out of the target of 125 lakhs 16.17 lakhs had been advanced through Central Co-operative banks. In all 2907 beneficiaries (non-farm) were benefited.

Long-term Loans

Long term loans Rs. 86 lakhs had been disbursed to 80 beneficiaries by Land Development Bank for purchase of tractors, mini-lorries and other small transporting vehicles. Match factories are also the beneficiaries of the long term loans.

Professionals (Doctors, Engineers, Dentists, ENT's, were disbursed Rs. 18.6 lakhs benefiting 37 persons.The target was Rs. 28.3 lakhs. Fall below the target. 171 persons received housing loans received Rs. 248.71 lakhs.

Through TANFED Rs. 324.70 lakhs worth chemical fertilizers, pesticides, seeds and agricultural implements were issued. It is against the target Rs. 594 lakhs. 1700 farmers were benefited.

The district consumer co-operative whole sale societies, co-ops. marketing societies, primary co-operative stores, Students co-operative stores, PACBs' put together had advanced Rs. 2946.97 lakhs till Oct. 31, 98. It is against the target of Rs. 5400 lakhs.

Fair-price Shops

The co-operatives run 591 fair-price shops. Out of that 421 shops sustained losses. It even after receiving a subsidy of Rs. 35,18,816.

Deposit Mobilisation

PACB's - Rs. 880 Lakhs.

70 PACB have safe rooms.

The story of co-operatives is not a good one to follow as Tuticorin is concerned. Unlike, it's counterpart Virudunagar it has failed to show any signs success in traditional fields, as Virudunagar district. We can see the achievements are far below the targets.

It has no multi-dimensional growth as Virudunagar district.

The Health co-operative are unique in Virudunagar.The women run fair-price shops are unique to Virudunagar distt. The Thiruthangap Co-op. Credit Society runs on it's own funds, even without aid from either NABARD or Central co-operatives.

Unlike, Virudunagar the back drop of Tuticorin district is Urban based. Probably, the needs of co-operatives is more for rural than urban. A study may be made in future.

Co-operatives—A New Dimension

The aim of co-operatives is the change the life of people in rural areas. Many mistake the area of co-operation is limited farm loans and inputs.

A new kind of co-operatives are emerging in the country. Now people themselves organise and indulge in development works. The Work Banks says that the crux of success in development activity depends on people's participation. In future only such type of co-operatives should be encouraged to get maximum results at minimum cost.

Here is an Example (Case study)

Water is the key to rural development. Mere application of fertilizers, pesticides and use of machinery cannot grow corn unless water is available. The main reason for poverty in villages is the non-availability of water.

Human Development Index stress the need of it for human and animal consumption. The co-op. banks may disburse cattle loan under "Operation Flood" to rear milching animals. Who will provide water and fodder for animals. Is there may body working on the primary need?

If there is any movement with people's participation; we call it as co-operative movement. They work for a common need. Put their resources together. If it is not called as co-operation then what else.

Kansalbail village set an example. The village is in Dharampuri disuict of Tamilnadu, a dry belt surrounded by hills. In near Palacode at a cost of Rs.13 lakhs a water conservation scheme was started. It was started under Land Resource Conservation. Now 100 hectares is to be benefited. Tamilnadu afforestation project-water augmentation scheme initiated the project.

According to the forest department 100 odd house in the village depend on agriculture. The related activities kept their life going.

Hence, augmenting water was the major economic development activity in the village.

How they did it ?

The pond-cum construction of check dams at a cost of Rs. 21

lakhs (98) It irrigated all the lands and recharged well-water levels. 10 wells derived the indirect benefit of the project.

In addition, the tank water was taken to the fields directly without pumping water due gravitational force. Otherwise the farmers would have used oil or electrical motor for pumping. The check dam at a higher level saved energy.

A few farmers without wells get water directly from the check-dam. The pecolation of water has solved the problem of drinking water.

Besides, villagers have formed a 10 members watershed committee which controlled optimum utilisation of water. People have changed from dry crops to wet crops.

The biggest achievement for the forest department is of the local people in protecting the forest from cattle damage and biotic intereferences.

Just 10 months after people's commitment the forest has become dense. Many other development efforts fail to get the desired benefits. Water augmentation alone could get all the benefits - Says Mr. Paulraj, District Forest Officer of Dharmapuri district. The above scheme is the brain-child of the Forest Department of Dharmapuri district. Officer with commitment could do wonders in development. It is a perfect example.

Now they have water throughout the year. They have three crops a year. Rear cattle.

Forest department people are like unsung heros of the war. They fight against poverty in remote regions. Out 'hats-Off' to those people (forest department personnel) for their commitment.

Encouraged by success they plan to construct three more check dams in surrounding villages.

New Forms of Co-operative

A case study of Thanjavur district.

District Rural Development Agency is taking steps to develop agriculturally developed and Industrial underdeveloped Thanjavur district. It involves people's participation. The scheme is called NAMAKU NAME (we for ourselves).

For this scheme people will comfard to do the development work using their own funds and funds with M.L.A's and M.P's of the area.

Government has allotted Rs. 25 lakhs for M.L.A's and Rs. 1 crore for the M.P.'s to spent in their areas.

With that money roads have been built, bridges constructed, infrastructure facilities provided in schools, villages are provided with water and electricity.

Now 589 Panchayaths were benefited by the scheme. Sri. T.N. Ramanthan and T.R. Vedhanayagam (District Collector and Project Officer, respectively) have taken keen interest.

Now 18 schemes both individual oriented and community oriented are in operation. Under individual oriented scheme houses are constructed, loans given for the purchase of milch animals. (IRDP).

Training in putting up street lights, construction of roads, bridges, providing basic infrastructure; building for public distribution system, community halls, toilets in schools are done under Training for Rural Youth Self Employment scheme.

Under 'Namku Name' scheme a road was laid between Melayur and Katchikattu village, Puzhchanallur, Kothukoil in Thiruvidamaruthus Panchayath Union. The total cost of road was Rs. 8.6 lakhs. People's contribution is Rs. 2.16 lakhs.

People pay money a part of the expenditure met to provide infrastructure. It is called as Participatory development. It is case of co-operation where the beneficiaries directly participate and also contribute.

Under this scheme the public money is spent carefully and at the same time people also participate.

Co-operation should not be merely government induced and carried by officials.

In some case when people themselves do Government may help the financially.

People (beneficiaries) alone know what they want. When their money is involved they take care that it is utilised judicially.

References

1. Materials provided by the Co-operative Department of Virudunagar.
2. Hindu; 26 No. 98 (On Tuticorin dt)
3. The Hindu; dated 11-12-98. (On namaku name)
4. The Hindu, dated 24th Dec., 1998.

9

Co-operative Audit in Tamil Nadu

*Prof. (Dr.) V. Rengaswamy**
and Dr. R. S. Mani **

The audit of the accounts of a Co-operative Society becomes necessary in order to protect the common interest of its members and to guard the society against frauds and irregularities. The audit helps to assess the credit-worthiness of the society by the creditors and guards the society against possible mismanagement and failure. Co-operative audit is necessary to protect the interest of investors and to maintain the right image in the minds of the public.

Meaning

Co-operative audit is an application of the general principles of auditing to the examination of accounts of a Co-operative Society. According to Dr. O. R. Krishnaswami, Co-operative audit is an examination of accounts and an enquiry into the affirms of a society in order to ascertain the correctness of accounts and the extent to which the activities of the society have been useful in promoting the socio-economic welfare of its members through the satisfaction of their needs in accordance with the principles of co-operation.[1]

Objectives of Co-operative Audit

The objectives of co-operative audit are:

1. To ascertain the correctness of accounts
2. To detect the prevent errors and frauds
3. To examine whether the affairs of the society have been carried on in accordance with the principles of co-operation

* Prof. Rengaswamy, P.G. Dept. of Commerce Madurai—Kamraj University
**Dr. Mani, Dept. of Commerce, Yadava College (Autonomous), Madurai (Tamil Nadu).

and the provisions of co-operative law and

4. To assess the extent to which the conditions of the members have been improved by the activities of the society.

The Tamil Nadu Co-operative Societies Act, 1983 states that audit should be completed within a period of six months from the close of the co-operative year concerned. Further, the audit should include the following:

1. an examination of overdue debts if any,
2. verification of cash balance and securities of the society and
3. valuation of the assets and liabilities of the society.

According to Section 80(7) of the Act, if the results of the audit disclose any defect, the society concerned should take steps to remedy the defects disclosed, within three months from the date of communication of the results of the audit. The action taken in this regard should be reported to the Director of Co-operative Audit.

Difference between Audit of Co-operatives and Audit of Joint Stock Companies

In a Joint Stock Company, an auditor is appointed by shareholders to carry out an independent examination of the financial position and profits earned and report the results to them. The auditors of a Co-operative Society are appointed by the Government to ensure that the Co-operative Society is working and developing on sound lines in accordance with the principles of co-operation.

A Joint stock company is mainly a profit-seeking concern. The audit is done to disclose the profits available for dividend. But, in a Co-operative Society, the primary concern of audit is to ascertain how far the society has been following regulations and promoting the material and moral well-being of its members.

The auditors of companies are not expected to cover administrative audit, whereas the auditors of a Co-operative Society are expected to point out infringements of the Co-operative Societies Act, the Rules, the registered Bye-laws and the subsidiary regulations.

According to the Indian Companies Act, an auditor of a company has the right to access at all time to the books and accounts and vouchers of the company only. On the other hand, an auditor of a Co-operative Society has free access to the books, accounts and documents and also to cash, securities and other properties belonging to the society.

An auditor of a company is entitled to receive any information from the directors and officers of the company which is necessary for the purpose of audit. But, the Co-operative auditor is entitled to receive information regarding the transactions and working of the society from the past and present officers, employees and members of the society concerned.

A Co-operative auditor has powers to summon any person in possession of books, accounts and documents of the society and ask him to produce the same at any place either at the head-quarter of the society or at any branch for the purpose of audit. An auditor of a company has no such powers.

An auditor of a company is required to submit his audit report to the members of the company whereas an auditor of a Co-operative Society submits his report to the Co-operative Audit Department, which in turn sends it to the society concerned and to the Government.

A company auditor does not act as a valuer, whereas a co-operative auditor is required to make valuation and verification of the assets and liabilities.

An auditor of a Co-operative Society is specially required to conduct an examination of overdue debts. But, in the case of audit of a company, there is no such specific requirement.

Co-operative Audit Practices

According to Section 80 (i) of the Tamil Nadu Co-operative Societies Act, 1983, every registered society should be audited at least once in every co-operative year.[2]

The Director of Co-operative Audit arranges for the audit of co-operative societies in the state of Tamil Nadu through his subordinate officers working at the district and circle levels.

Every co-operative society should pay to the Government of Tamil Nadu, the fee for the audit of its accounts, as fixed by the Director of Co-operative Audit.

Every registered co-operative society should prepare its financial statements and keep them ready for audit within three months from the end of the co-operative year. If the financial statements are not prepared and if there are valid reasons for the delay, the Registrar has the power to extend the period for preparing the financial statements for audit upto six months.

The audit should be completed within six months from the close of the co-operative year. If the audit of a society could not be completed within six months from the close of the co-operative year, the Director of Co-operative Audit has powers to extend this period beyond six months, subject to a maximum of six months in the aggregate if there are valid reasons for the same. The reasons must be stated in writing.

The financial and administrative aspects of co-operative societies are audited to ensure that they are functioning in accordance with the co-operative principles, Acts, Rules and bye-laws.

Organisational Structure of Co-operative Audit in Tamil Nadu

The Organisational Structure & Co-operative Audit in Tamil Nadu consists of the Directorate of Co-operative Audit at the State level, 3 Regional Co-operative Audit Offices at Madurai, Coimbatore and Madras and the District Co-operative Audit Offices at the district level. Normally there is a only one district co-operative audit office in each district. In cash if the district is big, there are two district co-operative audit offices, as in Madras, Chengalpet, South Arcot, Thanjavur, Salem, Madurai and Chimbaranar Districts. There are 28 district co-operative audit offices in Tamil Nadu.

For administrative convenience, a district is divided into number of circles with co-operative audit offices. The field staff like Senior Co-operative Auditors and Junior Co-operative Auditors are attached to each circle office to audit the lower level co-operative Societies.

Director of Co-operative Audit

Since 17th June, 1981, the Director of Co-operative Audit has been made the Head of the Co-operative Audit Department in Tamil Nadu. He is in the cadre of the Joint Secretary of Finance, Government of Tamil Nadu. The Co-operative Audit Department is under the control of the Finance Department, Government of Tamil Nadu. Figure 9.1 shows the Organisational Structure of Co-operative Audit Department in Tamil Nadu.

The co-operative department is functioning from the Secretariat of the Government of Tamil Nadu. In the office of the Director of Co-operative Audit, the Director is assisted by a Chief Audit Officer

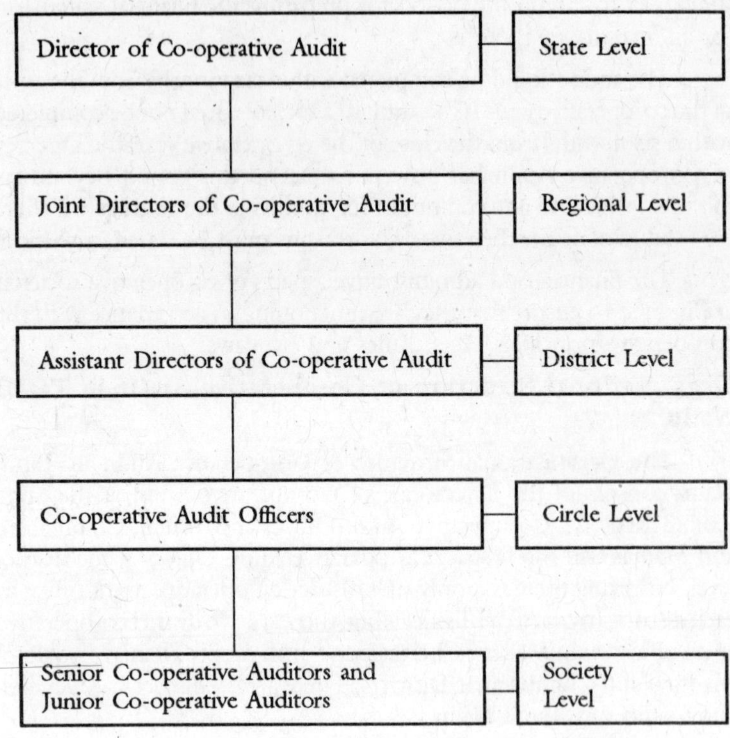

Fig. 9.1 : Organisational Structure of Co-operative Audit in Tamil Nadu

and a Deputy Chief Audit Officer. The Deputy Chief Audit Officer acts as a personal assistant to the Director of Co-operative Audit. Apart from this, there are superintendents, office assistants and last grade servants to help the Director of Co-operative Audit to discharge his duties effectively.

The Director of Co-operative Audit issues audit certificates to all apex level co-operative institutions in the state, district central co-operative banks, co-operative spinning mills, co-operatives sugar mills and the like. He also issues audit certificates to all co-operative societies where the Joint Registrars of Co-operative Societies function as special officers.

The Director of Co-operative Audit reviews the audit reports sent by the District Co-operative Audit Offices. He reviews the progress of co-operative audit in various regions while on tour, and discusses the same with the auditors to find out the reasons for the delay in completing the audit work, if any. The Director also makes surprise visits to societies and verifies cash balances and checks the stocks. He inspects the district co-operative audit offices once a year to review the work done by them.

Joint Director of Co-operative Audit

There are three Regional Co-operative Audit Offices functioning at Madurai, Coimbatore and Madras. In order to control and coordinate the audit personnel and to facilitate timely completion of audit, the Co-operative Audit Department in Tamil Nadu had been divided into three regions with their head quarters at Madurai, Coimbatore and Madras. The Regional Officer links the state level and district level audit offices. The Regional Co-operative Audit Office is headed by a Joint Director of Co-operative Audit.

The Joint Director of Co-operative Audit performs the following functions:

1. He is the leave sanctioning authority for the auditors working in the region who want to avail themselves of leave for more than 30 days.
2. He inspects the District Co-operative Audit Offices in the region.
3. He issues audit certificates to Co-operative Societies managed by the officers at the level of the Deputy Registrar of co-operative Societies.
4. He prepares budget estimates for the region and sends it to the Director of Co-operative Audit.

The district-wise jurisdiction of the three Regional Officers of Co-operative Audit Department in Tamil Nadu is shown in Table 9.1.

Assistant Director of Co-operative Audit

The District Co-operative Audit Office is headed by an Officer in the cadre of the Assistant Director of Co-operative Audit. At present, there are 28 district level audit offices in Tamil Nadu. The Assistant director of Co-operative audit is in charge of audit work in the respective district concerned.

The Assistant Director of Co-operative Audit performs the following functions:

1. He approves the consolidated audit programmes of the co-operative societies in the district.

Table 9.1 : Audit Regions in Tamil Nadu

Sl. No.	*Name of the Region*	*Name of the District in the Region*	*Total No. of Units in the Region*
1.	Madurai	Madurai, Periyakulam, Trichirappalli, Pudukkottai, Dindigul, Sivaangai, Virudhunagar, Kovilpatti, Tuticorin, Tirunelveli and Nagarcoil	12
2.	Coimbatore	Coimbatore, Erode, Oothagamandalam, Salem, Nammakkal, Dharmapuri, Vellore and Tiruvannamali	8
3.	Madras	Madras (North), Madras (South) Tiruvallur, Kancheepuram, Villupuram, Cuddalore, Tanjavur and Kumbakonam.	8
	Total		28

2. He periodically reviews the audit work of the societies at the district level.
3. He issues audit certificates to the co-operative societies in the district for which audit has been completed.
4. He conducts test audit for the co-operative societies in the district and maintains a list of societies for which test audit has been done during each year. He sends the test audit report to the Director of Co-operative Audit.

Co-operative Audit Officer

Each district is divided into a number of circle co-operative audit offices. Each circle co-operative audit office is headed by a co-operative audit officer. The Circle Co-operative Audit Officers plans the audit for the circle and deputes the manpower for the same. He is assisted by the field staff such as Senior Co-operative Auditors and Junior Co-operative Auditors. He regulates the audit work in the circle and reviews the work done by the field staff.

The Circle Co-operative Audit Officer decides the number of societies to be audited by each field staff in consultation with the District Co-operative Audit Officer. The Circle Co-operative Audit Officer prepares the audit programme of the society in his circle and it is sent to the District Co-operative Audit Officer for approval and implementation. He deputes the Senior Co-operative Auditors and the Junior Co-operative Auditors for conducting concurrent audit.

The Circle Co-operative Audit Officer issues audit certificates to all the Primary Agricultural Co-operative Banks and also conducts the test audit.

Senior Co-operative Auditors and Junior Co-operative Auditors

The Senior Co-operative Auditors and Junior Co-operative Auditors are the actual persons who conduct audit in the co-operative societies.

The duties of the co-operative Auditor are given below:

a) He shall examine the overdue debts.

b) He shall verify the cash and securities and

c) He shall make a valuation of the assets and liabilities of the society.[3]

He should submit the audit report in the prescribed form. He makes sure that the balance sheet gives a true and fair view of the state of societies affairs on that date and the profit and loss account gives a true and fair view of the profit or loss of the society for the year.

Powers of the Co-operative Auditors

The following are the statutory powers of the auditors of the co-operative department:

1. The Co-operative auditors have free access to all the books, accounts, documents, papers, securities, cash and other properties belonging to or in the custody of the society.
2. The auditor has powers to summon any person in possession or responsible for the custody of societies documents and to produce the same at any place, the head quarters of the society or any branch thereof.
3. The auditor has the right to receive the required information in regard to the transactions and working of the society from every officer, employee, past or present member of the society.
4. The auditor has the right to attend the annual general body meeting of the society with which he is concerned as a co-operative auditor.

Review Meetings

The Assistant Director of Co-operative Audit conducts review meeting for ascertaining the progress of audit. He conducts two meetings every month, one for the Co-operative Audit Officers and the other for the Senior Co-operative Auditors and Junior co-operative Auditors. The Assistant Director of Co-operative Audit also reviews the progress in the collection of audit fees, observance of fundamental rules, audit cost and the vacancy position of auditors. He makes an elaborate discussion with the audit staff for improving the performance of audit. The review meetings help to find out the reasons for the delay in completing the audit reports, problems encountered and steps to be taken for speedy completion of audit reports.

Conclusion

The Co-operative audit is different from company audit. The Co-operative auditor has wider powers to summon any person in possession or responsible for the custody of documents and produce the same at any place of the society. Every registered society should be audited in every co-operative year. The Director of co-operative audit arranges for the audit of co-operative societies in Tamil Nadu through his subordinate officers working at district and circle levels. The financial and administrative aspects of the co-operative societies are audited. The audit should be completed within six months from the close of the co-operative year.

References

1. "The Synopsis of Co-operative Audit"—Refresher Classes, The Tamil Nadu Kotturavu Thanikkai Aluvalar Sangam, Madras, May 1987, p.1.
2. The Co-operative Societies Act, 1983, Government of Tamil Nadu. p.72.
3. Dr. O. R. Krishnaswami, opp. cit., p.40.

10

Role of LAMPS for the Development of Tribals in Orissa

*Dr. S. N. Tripathy**

As per 1991 census, Orissa has more than 70.32 lakhs tribal population constituting 22.21 percent of the total population. It is found from various census reports that though in terms of absolute numbers the tribal population has been increasing, but the percentage of tribals to total population of the State has been decreasing from 24.07 percent in 1961 to 23.11 percent in 1971 and to 22.43 percent in 1981 which finally to 22.31 percent in 1991, (Table 10.1). The undivided districts of Koraput, Mayurbhanj, Sundargarh, Kalahandi and Phulbani are mostly tribal concentrated.

Table 10.1 : Percentage of Tribal Population in Orissa as per Various Census Reports

Census Year	*Total Population*	*Tribal Population*	*Percentage of Tribal Population to the total population*
1961	17,548,846	42,23,757	24.07
1971	21,944,615	50,71,937	23.11
1981	26,370.271	59,15,067	22.43
1991	31,659,736	70,32,214	22.21

Source : Collected from various Census Reports.

* Dr. Tripathy belongs to the Department of Economics, Aska Science College, Aska, Orissa—761 111.

There are 62 types of tribes in Orissa, residing in the remote areas of forests, hills and naturally isolated regions. Most of the tribals in Orissa are much below the poverty line and thus, in the state of backwardness. These tribals perform a wide spectrum of activities ranging from food gathering and hunting to slash and burn cultivation (Podu or shifting cultivation), settled plough cultivation with occasional practices of cottage industries. The tribals of Orrisa, with slight variations have a highly egalitarian society, with high status for women and dignity of labour. They have maintained their values as manifested in their rites, rituals and traditional institutions, in spite of centuries of on slaught by external forces.

The Tribal Problems

Tribals in India, as well as in Orissa, have been experiencing diverse problems. Taking the advantage of their illiteracy, simplicity and ignorance, and the moneylenders, the middlemen and of the unscrupulous traders enter into the tribal regions and exploit them through various dubious means. Besides, they also confront the problem of land alienation, exorbitant rate of interest, wide-spread poverty and indebtedness, bondage, exploitation, leading to sale of child and starvation death.

These miseries of tribals accentuate due to rapid growth of population, pressure on landholding, illiteracy, deforestation, inadequate infrastructural and social service facilities etc. Even some of the tribals are uprooted from their native abodes either due to displacement by non-tribals or due to establishment of major industrial and irrigation projects.

Co-operative Approach for Tribal Development

To eliminate the age old exploitation and repression of tribals in different economic activities, sincere efforts have been made by the Government in building up co-operative structure in the tribal economy during the plan period in India. Many commissions, committees, study teams and working groups have repeatedly been emphasised the significance of co-operativization of tribal economy in the country. In its report, the social welfare team of the committee on plan projects (1959) recommended that, "Commercial exploitation of forests be entrusted to co-operatives rather than to contractors." The Dhebar Commission (1961) recommended that "the sale and marketing of the produce and supply of tribal peoples' requirements at reasonable price should receive special attention through co-operatives. A special working group on

Co-operation (1961) attributed the slow development of Co-operative movement in tribal areas to structural defects, management problems, faulty procedures and business methods. The group suggested a separate organizational set up for promotion of co-operative ideas among the tribal communities, so as to provide such services as were being rendered by private traders and further, recommended the formation of an "Integrated Service Co-operative Society" at haat level. As a result of the recommendations of the working Group, State Governments set up Forest Labour Co-operative societies and multi-purpose co-operative societies and State level Tribal Development Corporations. Further, to improve the operational efficiency of co-operatives in Tribal Areas, Committee on co-operative structure in Tribal Areas under the Chairmanship of K. S. Bawa (1971) has recommended for the Chairmanship of the Large Scale Adivasi Multi-purpose Societies (LAMPS) by amalgamating service co-op. societies (SCS) in tribal areas which include package of service for tribal people. The main components of this package are credit (both production and consumption), supply of seeds and other agricultural inputs, marketing of agricultural and minor forest produce and supply of consumer goods. The committee recommended that a tribesman should not be required to approach too many institutions for assistance and the co-operative structure should essentially provide integrated credit and other services at one point. They suggested for creation of LAMPS at block level with branches at G.P. Head quarters or at important weekly market/Haat centres. For credit purposes the LAMPS have to be serviced by the Central Co-operative Banks (CCB), for supply of inputs and marketing and agricultural produce to the Regional Co-operative Marketing Society (RCMS) and for marketing of minor forest produce (MFP) to the Tribal Development Co-operative Society.

A detailed picture of the membership covered by LAMPS in Orissa during the period 1989-90 to 1994-95 has been presented in the Table 10.2. It is revealed from the table that the membership of the LAMPS in Orissa has increased from 808 thousands to 906 thousands during the said period. The participation of tribals in the total membership is about 58 percent.

Credit Flow

Credit is an essential input for the development of tribal agriculture. The LAMPS Supply short-term and Medium terms loans for agricultural purposes alongwith some amount of consumption loans.

Table 10.2 : Statement Showing Membership of LAMPS in Orissa

Year	*No. of LAMPS*	*Membership (in thousand)*			*Total Membership*
		ST	*SC*	*Others*	
1989–90	223	472 (58.41)	116	220	808
1990–91	223	482 (57.43)	120	230	832
1991–92	223	489 (57.73)	124	234	847
1992–93	223	510 (58.28)	127	238	875
1993–94	223	512 (57.65)	130	246	888
1994–95	223	519 (57.28)	132	255	906

Source : Collected from various Census Reports.

The detailed position regarding the advancement of loans by LAMPS has been exhibited in the Table 10.3. It is depicted from the Table that the percentage of short-term loans during the period 1989-90 to

Table 10.3 : The Advancement of Loans by LAMPS in Orissa

(Rs. in Lakhs)

Year	*Short-term Loans*	*Medium-term Loan*	*Total loan Outstanding*
1989–90	273 (7.54)	30 (0.82)	3617
1990–91	541 (23.46)	8 (0.34)	2306
1991–92	466 (25.28)	71 (3.85)	1843
1992–93	719 (35.75)	166 (8.25)	2011
1993–94	1084 (46.32)	495 (19.87)	2340
1994–95	1359 (47.88)	440 (15.64)	2838

Source : Office of the R.C.S., Orissa, Bhubaneswar.

Note : Figures in the parenthesis indicate the percentage to the total.

1994-95 marks an increasing trend. It has increased 7.54 percent to 47.88 period during the said period. Similarly, the flow of medium-term loans shows an increasing trend as it has registered a sharp rise from 0.82 percent in the 1989-90 to 1991-92. However, from 1992-93 onwards it registers a rising trend. The probable reason for increasing total outstanding loans during the said period may be due to non-repayment of loans because of failure of crops, natural calamities and lack of employment.

Further, the position of total loans over-due reveals a disheartening picture (Table 10.4). The scheduled castes and scheduled tribes combinedly held approximately more than 50 per cent of the loans. Exclusively, the tribals held about 40 percent of loans over-due. This speaks in volumes about the magnitude of poverty prevailing in the tribal areas.

Table 10.4 : Position of Loans Overdue
(Both Short-term and Medium-term Loans)

(Rs. in lakhs)

Year	*Total Loan Overdue*	*Total ST+SC Loan Overdue*	*Loans Over-due by Scheduled Tribe*	*Loans Over-due by Scheduled Castes*
1989–90	2592	1429 (55.13)	1103 (42.55)	326 (12.57)
1990–91	1449	823 (56.79)	625 (43.13)	198 (13.66)
1991–92	1209	627 (55.91)	517 (42.76)	159 (13.15)
1992–93	1321	597 (45.19)	416 (31.49)	181 (13.70)
1993–94	1262	645 (51.10)	474 (37.55)	171 (13.57)
1994–95	1431	761 (53.17)	577 (40.32)	184 (12.85)

Source : Office of the R.C.S., Orissa, Bhubaneṣwar.
Note : Figures in the parenthesis indicate the percentage to the total.

It is found from the Table 10.5 that there has been fluctuation in collection of tribal agricultural produce by the LAMPS. Generally, the tribals who are in the grip of unemployment and poverty, borrow from the moneylenders and businessmen in order to meet their urgent needs. Therefore, they are compelled to sale their products at a distressed price to such unscrupulous traders and middlemen. The value of Agricultural produce marketed by LAMPS in the year 1991-92 was as high as Rs. 774 lakhs. The important agricultural produces procured by LAMPS are maize, Jowar, Ragi, Blackgram, Mustard seeds, Niger seeds etc.

Table 10.5 : Marketing of Surplus Agricultural Produce (SAP) through LAMPS in Orissa

(Rs. in lakhs)

Year	*Agricultural produce marketed*
1989–90	54
1990–91	371
1991–92	774
1992–93	251
1993–94	62
1994–95	121

Source : As stated in Table 10.4.

However, with regard to marketing of agricultural produces of tribals, the LAMPS fail to procure the produce adequately from them as the tribals apprehend the adjustment of their agricultural produce towards their loan overdues. Therefore, it has been observed that the private traders and middlemen could procure more than eighty percent of the tribal agricultural produce and thereby exploit the tribals though distressed payment.

A perusal of the aforesaid analysis brings to light that even though the LAMPS have played a vital role in the advancement of credit cum marketing of products, it is indispensable to bring the tribals under co-operative fold for relieving them from the clutches of the private money lenders-Cum-traders. Because of the tribals fail to receive a fair and remunerative return for their products and if the exploitive elements continue to deny them the fruits of their labour, mere increase of the financial resources in five year plans for tribal welfare and execution of tribal development programmes may not benefit them to the extent contemplated. Therefore, there should be a proper coordination of institutional agencies like Agency marketing co-operative society, Tribal Development Co-operative corporations, State Marketing Federation etc. through supply of money to LAMPS. The tribal development strategy should be an integrated strategy combing the development of credit-Cum-Marketing facilities, infrastructural development, development of education, removal of exploitation of middlemen through payment of support prices to the tribals, provision of adequate employment and finally, to the active involvement of tribals in the process of development.

References

1. Tripathy, S.N., Marketing Co-operatives for tribal Development, Social Welfare, November, 1998.
2. Tripathy, S.N., Bonded Labour in India, Discovery Publishing House, New Delhi, 1989.
3. Tripathy, S.N., Impact of Road Transport in Tribal India, Discovery Publishing House, New Delhi, 1994.
4. Tripathy, S.N., Co-operatives for Rural Development, Discovery Publishing House, New Delhi, 1998.

11

Co-operatives and Fisheries Development

with Special Reference to Districts of Faizabad and Ambedkar Nagar (U.P.)

*Prof. A. C. Pandey**
*Prof. J. P. Mishra***

Introduction

Fisheries and aquaculture is a growing industry in the twin districts of Faizabad and Ambedkar Nagar. One interesting aspect of this industry is that it represents an early shift from wild capture fisheries to a farm-produces fishery, similar to much earlier shifts to farm-produced food from hunted food. The two sister districts have average annual, fish production of 1900 kg/ha from culture ponds and 100 kg/ha from reservoirs. The potential of freshwater ponds and reservoirs suitable for aquaculture is 4009.50 and 19.64 ha, respectively. While technology is necessary condition for the development of scientific aquaculture the economics and required profitability is the sufficient condition for aquaculture development through diffusion and adoption of technologies. Various aspects of price-spread and status of fisheries in these districts have already is reported by Pandey and Mishra (1998) and Pandey (1999). This paper is designed to examine the present status and role of fish cooperatives in the development of fisheries and aquaculture in general, and districts of Faizabad and Ambedkar Nagar in particular.

* Department of Fisheries, Narendra Deva University of Agriculture and Technology, Kumarganj, Faizabad—224 229, U.P. and

** Department of Agricultural Economics, Narendra Deva University of Agriculture and Technology, Kumarganj, Faizabad—224 229, U.P.

General Scenario

Even after celebrating 50th year of Independence, nearly half of the population is poor and half of our culturable land has also remained poor. Though the country is endowed with rich natural resources like water, minerals, sun-shine, temperature or all sorts of climates, cattle and fisheries wealth, and manpower, we have not so far been able to adequately utilise these resources. During five decades, the century and state of U.P. have made progress in several spheres including industry, aquaculture, agriculture, education, science, technology, social welfare, and many others. However, only a privileged few have taken advantage of this. Economic and social disparities have been widening and the free market economy may further accentuate the situation.

The cooperative movement which received legal sanctity during 1904 can play a dynamic role in achieving our objectives. During the past 94 years, cooperative movement has entered several sectors like credit, banking, processing, housing, warehousing, irrigation, transport and industries. It is because of credit cooperatives that it was possible to weaken the strong hold of money lenders on thousands of poor families and free them their bondage. Dairy and sugar cooperative have made us a major nation in the world in milk and sugar production.

Parameter of Cooperative

A cooperative is an autonomous association of persons united voluntarily to meet their common economic social and cultural needs and aspirations through a jointly owned and democratically controlled enterprise. It is intentionally wide in scopes, recognising that individual members of the various cooperatives will be involved differently and that they must have some freedom in how they organise their affairs. The basic norms of the cooperatives are voluntary and open membership; democratic control; member's economic participation; autonomy and independence; provision to educate, train and provide information to members; cooperation amongst cooperatives and concern for community.

Dynamic Direction

Unemployment, underemployment and denial of adequate income to enjoy the basic minimum needs, is the real challenge before the country. For want of a national network of market system, the agriculture; horticultural; and aquaculture produces have remained the usual suffers. Many times to produce more has become a crime; there is no adequate protection against the vagaries of nature. India is endowed with natural resources. There is tremendous scope for development of aquaculture and fisheries and many related activities. Efforts by individuals are too limited to carry these activities on a massive scale. As already established by sugar and dairy cooperative, it is now necessary to give a new orientation and direction to cooperatives working in fisheries and aquaculture, and various related industries. This approach has become for more imperative view of the free market economy and the global competition.

National Cooperative Development Corporation and Fisheries Sector

At national level an apex institution known as National Cooperative Development Corporation (NCDC) has been promoting and developing fisheries cooperative since 1974 after amendment of its Act to include fisheries within its purview. The NCDC provides assistance to fisherman cooperatives on liberal terms for the following programmes— *i*) purchase of operational implements such as fishing boats, nets, engines, trawlers, etc., *ii*) creation of marketing infrastructure facilities for transport vehicles, godowns, retail outlets, etc., *iii*) establishment of fish processing units such as ice plants, cold storage, etc. *iv*) development of fish hatcheries and farms in inland areas, *v*) preparation of feasibility reports, *vi*) integrated fisheries development projects (IFDP) for marine, brackish-and inland water including components of fishing inputs, infrastructure facilities, marketing, training extension, contingencies, etc., *vii*) appointment of experts under "Technical and Promotional Cell Scheme", and viii) installation of computers for management, monitoring of programmes.

Assistance from NCDC

The NCDC has sanctioned Rs. 247.02 crores (Rs. 151.24 crores already released) for development of fisheries through co-operatives upto March 31, 1996.

Since 1985-86, the NCDC has been providing training, educating member fishermen and creating infrastructure for production, storage, processing and marketing of fish under IFDP. As on March 31, 1996, the NCDC has assisted IFDP in coastal states at a block cost of Rs. 165.62 crores involving NCDC's assistance of Rs. 151.66 crores. More than 80,000 fishermen have been targeted to be benefited from all the IFDP, these projects envisage an estimated additional fish production of over 2.50 lakh t/yr. The NCDC has been able to recover 50-75 per cent of loan under various projects. Beneficiary fisherman are more efficient and earn more income than non-beneficiaries by spending equal or less number of days in fishing. About 69 per cent of beneficiary fisherman and 48 per cent of non-beneficiary fisherman have opined that fisheries cooperative societies auctioners fetch better prices than private auctioners.

The NCDC has proposed an outlay of Rs. 220.00 crores for the 9th Plan period for fisheries cooperative societies (Anonymous, 1996) under different schemes (Table 11.1).

Table 11.1 : Details of Fisheries Co-operative Societies in Faizabad and Ambedkar Nagar Districts

Co-operative Name and Address	*No. of members*	*Members covered under insurance*	*Details of Activities*		
			River	*Lake/ pond etc.*	*Area*
1. PFCS, Magalsi, Sohawal	105	105	Saryu	------	35 km.
2. PFCS, Ramdih Sarai, Basakhari	35	35	----	Lake-1	115.0 ha
3. PFCS, Nirmitni Bhiyano	60	56	----	Lake-1	30.0 ha
4. PFCS, Katehari Bhiti, Hath Pakad	74	----	----	Pond-4	11.50 ha
5. PFCS, Miranpur, Akabarpur	65	65	----	Pond-4	3.75 ha
6. PFCS, Masada Mohanpur, Hajan Patti.	66	----	-----	Lake-1	52.0 ha
7. PFCS, Barahata Majha, Pura Bazar	51	51	----	Pond-1	1.8 ha
8. PFCS, Maya Bazar, Goshaiganj	60	52	----	Pond-1	3.0 ha
9. PFCS, Chaheta Ghat, Chahoda Shahpur	93	61	Saryu	Boat Ferry	-----
10. PFCS, Faizabad city	90	22	Saryu	Fish-sell	-----
11. PFCS, Bukia Pahalwan, Sandha	58	----	-----	Pond-1	77.2 ha.
12. PFCS, Ram Nagar, Faizabad Proposal submitted	--	--	----	----	----

Fisheries Cooperatives

On account of various development measures so far undertaken, the fish production has increased to 49.50 lakh during 1995–96 as compared to only 7.52 lakh during 1950–51. The potential of fish production is estimated to be 84 lakh t/yr. of which 45 lakh t could be from inland sector and 39 lakh t from marine sector. The fish consumption in the country and U.P. is 3.5 and 0.8 kg./capita/yr. respectively as against recommended quantity of 12.2 kg./capita/yr. by Indian Council of Medical Research (Pandey, 1995). The total domestic fish production in the year 1992–93 was worth Rs. 5860 crores and the export of fish and fishery products had fetched Rs. 3575.27 crores during 1994–95. Per capita/day consumption of fishery products of our country is only 1.6% as against the 28% of Japan.

There are 9,000 primary fishermen co-operative societies (PFCS) with 1139000 members covering about 21% of active fishermen in the country. Above these PFCS are 102 central co-operative societies at the district and regional levels and 11 co-operative federations at the state level. The top echelon is occupied by the National Federation of Fishermen's Co-operatives (FISHCOPFED). The districts of Faizabad and Ambedkar Nagar share 6 each of the PFCS (Table 11.2). A total of 734 PFCS (including 12 of the Faizabad and Ambedkar Nagar) have been registered all over the state of U.P.

Table 11.2 : The Proposed 9th Plan Outlay of NCDC for Fisheries Co-operatives

Scheme	*Proposed Outlay (in crores)*
1. Centrally sponsored scheme for co-operatives in co-operatively under-developed states/union territories	40.00
2. Centrally sponsored scheme for Reservoirs fisheries development	40.00
3. NCDC sponsored scheme for fisheries co-operatives in co-operatively developed states/union territories	40.00
4. NCDC sponsored scheme for IFDP's	100.00
Grand Total	220.00

Presently the co-operative structure differs from state to state. While Kerala has got a 2-tier system (village and apex) and the U.P. a 3-tier system (village, district and apex), the Maharashtra has 4-tier (village, district, regional and apex) system. Consensus is gradually emerging to develop 3-tier structure (Fig. 11.1), viz. PFCS at village level, central or secondary at the district level and the apex at state capital level. These societies play vital role in educating and improving socio-economic conditions of the fellow mebers, and inculcate a sense of cooperation among them. Eleven village ponds and 3 lakes have been leased to the PFCS of the Faizabad and Ambedkar Nagar districts for fish culture whereas different stretch of river Saryu have been leased to PFCS for boat-ferrying and capture fisheries (Table 11.2).

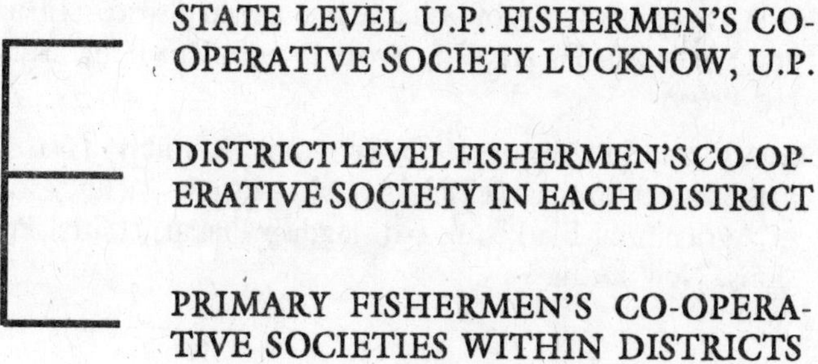

Fig. 11.1 : Three-tier System in Fishermen's Co-operative Society

Life of the majority of the members of the PFCS have been insured for Rs. 25000/- in the event of death and Rs. 12,500/- in case of permanent disability. A nominal annual premium of Rs. 11/- per member is shared by Provincial and Union Governments on behalf of the member fishermen.

Summary

Fisheries cooperatives are destined to play important role in enhancing the fish production and socio-economic conditions of the fishermen. The cooperative should be strengthened at the nation, district and village levels to fasten the process of development. Future growth in this sector will depend largely upon what happens to the demand for selected fishery products relative to the demand for protein sources, and on relative production costs.

Acknowledgments

We are grateful to Hon'ble Vice-Chancellor, Dean (Agriculture) and Professor & Head (Fisheries) for providing encouragement and facilities. Thanks are also due to Shri Ram Prakash Dubey for typing the manuscript.

References

Anonymous, 1996. Cooperative benefits fishermen. NCDC bulletin 30 : 6-8.

Pandey, A.C. 1995. Machhali Palan. Gram Vikas Prakashan. Lucknow, 125 pp.

Pandey, A.C., 1999. Status of Fisheries in the twin districts of Faizabad and Ambedkar Nagar, U.P. Proc. IVth Indian Fisheries Forum (In Press).

Pandey, A.C. and J.P. Mishra, 1998. Economic feasibility of fish culture in the district Faizabad (U.P.), India : A case study. In: Encyclopaedia of Agricultural Marketing (ed. Jagdish Prasad), Mittal Publications. New Delhi.

12

Evaluating Primary Handloom Weavers' Co-operative Societies

A Study in Orissa

*Radha Krishna Panda**

Thousands of years ago when the art of embalming was practised in ancient Egypt, the mummies were embalmed in India silk and court of Imperial Rome glittered with gold and silver brocades of Delhi, says Bansil (Cited by Jyoti Rani and Prema Kumari). The gossamer silk of Varanasi, fine Muslin of Dacca, Patola of Baroda, Sambalpuri or bandha sarees made by thè bhulias of Orissa etc. mark the historic significance of handloom industry in India. Basically handloom industry is a traditional cottage industry which contributed 21.29 percent of the total textile production and occupies third position after mills and powerloom sector (Economic Survey, 1997-98).

Handloom industry which thrives in the decentralised sector of the textile industry provide employment to about there million weavers and turns out product with special design and appeal (the Hindu Survey of Indian Industry). Further, Orissa consisting of 4,15,261 weavers population is able to generate total output worth of Rs. 8812.04 Lakhs with 1,19,005 looms in the year 1997 (Orissa Handloom Basic Facts, 1997).

Weavers who constitute the kingpin of handloom industry have entered into the fold of cooperation during 1940s. Indeed, Weavers' Cooperative Society is an institutional attempt to bring about the socio-economic transformation of the masses of weavers. By the end of 1997, out of the total 1,19005 looms, 1,10,124 looms (92.53%) have remained in the fold of cooperation (Annual Report of the Directorate

* Mr. Panda, Lecturer in Economics, Somnath Science College, Mundamarai Ganjam (Orissa)—761 114

of Textiles, 1997-98). At present there are about 840 primary Handloom Weavers Cooperative Societies (PHWCS) in Orissa which are more concentrated in the districts like Bargarh, Bolangir, Sonepur, Sambalpur, Cutack, Ganjam etc.

Assuming the greater significance of this industry, this paper makes an attempt to assess the performance of PHWCSs in Ganjam district of Orrisa. This district consisting of 26,318 weavers population runs 8535 looms by the year 1997 (Orissa Handloom Basic Facts, 1997).

To examine the performance of PHWCSs, factors like no. of profit/loss making PHWCSs, production trend, amount of sales, quantum of employment, price index and materials costs index béen studied on the basis of time-series data ranging from 1990-91 to 1997-98.

Scope and Delimitations of the Study

With a view to study the performance of PHWCSs, the district Ganjam has been selected purposefully. The selection of the district is made owing to the high concentration of weavers as well as the author's nativity. It is anticipated that some generations drawn on the basis of this study may be extended relating to the performance of PHWCSs in Orissa. Further, for the preparation of sales prices index and materials cost index, the study is delimited to the PHWCSs like. G. Damodarapalli and Mundamarai of the district under study.

Objectives of the Study

This study mainly highlights the following objectives:

i. To analyse the percentage share of Profit/Loss making PHWCSs in the district.

ii. To examine the production trend of PHWCSs in this district.

iii. To explain the volume of sales of all the PHWCSs in the district.

iv. To point-out of degree of correlation between sales and employment.

v. To study the price behaviour for the range of products produced by PHWCSs.

vi. To investigate the materials cost index of PHWCSs.

Methodology

a) Selection of Sample Area and Sample Items

Specifically designed to evaluate the performance of PHWCSs of

Ganjam district in Orissa, commodities like towel (Y-26), Dhoti (Y-26), Dhoti (Y-40), Saree (Y-40) and Saree (Y-26) have been choosen as the sample commodities out of a wide range of commodities. The selection of these items has been made as these products are common items produced by almost all the PHWCSs. Similarly, in order to study the materials costs index, the cost of labour, yarn and training for labour have been choosen.

b) Collection of Data

The study is mainly developed on the basis of secondary time series data which have been collected from the published booklets and leaflets of Directorate of Textiles (Orissa) and unpublished Official Records (audited) of Assistant Directorate of Textiles, Behrampur (Ganjam). Further, required time series data for the study fall under the study period from 1990-91 to 1997-98.

c) Techniques Used in the Study

After the collection of data, the study has been analysed and interpreted on the basis of different stastical techniques as outlined below:

i. The study takes into consideration the time series analysis where trend line is obtained with the help of least square formula.

ii. Weighted Price Index (Dorbish and Bowely's Method) has been used to calculate the sales price index.

iii. Simple Aggregative Method has been employed to examine the materials cost index.

iv. Simple arithmetic mean has been used to calculate the mean employment and mean unsold items during all the years under study.

v. Karl Pearson's co-efficient of correlation has been adopted to study the degree of correlation between employment and unsold stock.

vi. In the course of this study histograms have been used to illustrate different sets of data in the graphs.

Analysis of the Study

Performance of PHWCSs in terms of Profit and Loss

The number of Profit making PHWCSs, Loss making PHWCSs and no-profit/no loss making PHWCSs including their percentage share in the total PHWCSs in the district has been explained in Table 12.1 here below :

Table 12.1 : Performance of PHWCSs in Ganjam District

Year	*P*	*L*	*NP/ NL*	*Total*	*%P*	*%L*	*%NP/ NL*
1990–91	64	4	Nil	68	94.11	5.88	---
1991–92	64	4	Nil	68	94.11	5.88	---
1992–93	53	15	Nil	68	77.44	22.05	---
1993–94	52	12	01	65	80.00	18.46	1.53
1994–95	55	10	Nil	65	84.61	15.38	---
1995–96	57	8	Nil	65	87.69	12.30	---
1996–97	51	9	5	65	78.46	12.30	7.69
1997–98	N.A.	N.A.	N.A.	N.A.	N.A.	N.A.	N.A.

Source : Office of the Assistant Directorate of Textiles, Berhampur, Ganjam, Orissa.

N. B. :

P = No. of Profit making PHWCSs.
L = No. of Loss Making PHWCSs.
NP/PL : No. of No-profit/No loss Making PHWCSs
% P : Percentage of Profit Making PHWCSs
% L : Percentage of Loss Making PHWCSs
% NP/NL : Percentage of No-profit/No loss making PHWCSs

As per Table 12.1, the total numbers of PHWCSs of the area under study were 68 in the year 1990-91, 91-92 and 92-93 which declined to 65 in the subsequent years. In the eight years study period the number of profit making PHWCSs, shows declining trend, as it is evident from Table 12.1. In the year 1990-91, 94.11 percent of the total PHWCSs were enjoying profit which came down to 77.94 in the year 1992-93 and further declined to 78.46 percent in the year 1996-97. Further the percentage share of loss making units which was 5.11 percent in the year 1990-91, stood at 22.05 percent in the year 1992-93. It is better to mention that there has been continuous recovery in the loss making units in the subsequent years from 1993-94 to 1996–97. Thus either due to the patronage of Government or out of their in-built strength, the PHWCSs are reviving their position. In the year 1996-97, the number of NP/NL making PHWCSs is maximum at 5 and their percentage share was 7.69 as it is shown in Table 12.1.

As the number of profit making PHWCSs has declined from 64 in the year 1990-91 to 51 in the year 1996-97, the number of loss making PHWCSs and the number of NP/NL making PHWCSs have increased over years, therefore, on this ground the performance of these societies is not appreciable.

Production of PHWCSs

The value of clothes produced by all the PHWCSs operating in Ganjam district of Orissa has been explained in Table 12.2.

Table 12.2 : Production of PHWCSs

Years	*Production in Values (Lakhs)*	*Production Index Base Year : 1990 = 100*
1990	557.63	100.00
1991	519.31	93.12
1992	545.88	97.89
1993	616.11	110.48
1994	607.10	108.87
1995	746.98	133.95
1996	556.33	99.76
1997	439.34	78.78

Source : Office of the Assistant Directorate of Textiles, Berhampur.

It is evident from the data given in Table 12.2, that the value of clothes produced by all the PHWCSs in the study district was Rs. 557.63 lakh in the year 1990 which declined to Rs. 439.34 lakhs in 1997. Production Index suggests that there has been a fall in the total production to the extent of 21.9 percent in the year 1997 in comparison to the year 1990.

The production histogram (Fig. 12.1) shows the behaviour of total production of all PHWCSs in the Ganjam district. Further by fitting a linear trend, the production behaviour of PHWCSs has been ascertained. Table 12.3 shows the computation of linear trend.

Let the trend line be given by the equation $y = a+bx$

As the number of years under study are even, then,

$$x = \frac{t - (\text{Arithmatic mean of two middle years})}{1/2\ (\text{interval})}$$

Table 12.3 : Computation for Linear Trend

Years	*Production in Value (Rs. in lakhs) (Y)	$x=\frac{t-1993.5}{1/2}$	xy	x^2	Trend Value (in lakhs) Y = a+bx
1990	557.63	–7	–3903.41	49	530.42
1991	519.31	–5	–2792.94	25	545.68
1992	545.88	–3	–1637.64	9	556.84
1993	616.11	–1	616.11	1	568.00
1994	607.10	1	607.10	1	579.16
1995	746.98	3	2240.90	9	590.32
1996	556.33	5	2784.65	25	601.48
1997	439.34	7	3075.59	49	612.65
Total	$\Sigma y = 4588.71$	$\Sigma x = 0$	$\Sigma xy = 984.36$	$\Sigma x^2 = 168$	

Source : *Assistant Director of Textiles, Berhampur, Ganjam.

$$= \frac{t-(1993 + 1994)2}{1/2\,(1)}$$

$$= \frac{t-1993.5}{1/2}$$

Further the normal equations for estimating a and b of the assumed trend line are given by

$$\Sigma y = na + b\Sigma x$$

$$\Sigma xy = a\Sigma x + b\Sigma x^2$$

$$a = \Sigma y/n = 4588.71/8 = 573.58$$

$$b = \Sigma xy/\Sigma x^2 = 984.36/168 = 5.85$$

Substituting the values of a and b in the equation of trend line; we get

$$y = a + bx$$

$$= 573.58 + 5.58x$$

Putting x = –7, –5, –3, –1, 1, 3, 5 & 7 in the equation y = a+bx, the trend values of production of PHWCSs, for the years 1990 to 1997 are 530.42, 545.68, 556.84, 568.00, 579.16, 590.32, 601.48, 612.65

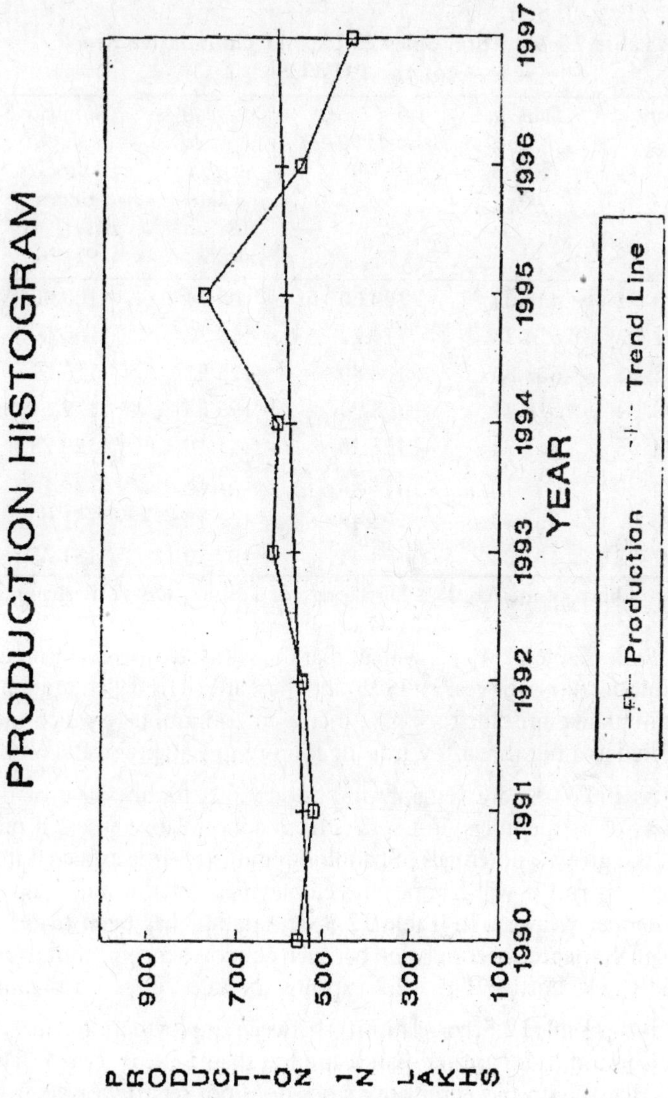

Fif. 12.1 : Production Histogram

respectively. Plotting these trend values, required trend line is fitted to the production histogram in Fig. 12.1. From the Fig. 12.1, it is marked that the total production of PHWCSs increases at a slower rate and 1995 onwards it falls decisively.

Table 12.4 : Total Sales & Unsold Cumulative Stock of the PHWCSs

Years	*Sales in Value (Rs. in lakhs)*	*Sales Index Base 1990–91 =100*	*Cumulative Unsold Stock in Value (Rs. in lakhs)*	*Cumulative Unsold Stock Index Base 1990–91=100*
1990–91	448.62	100.00	108.74	100.00
1991–92	514.28	114.72	113.77	104.62
1992–93	533.84	103.80	125.81	115.69
1993–94	528.21	98.94	195.35	179.64
1994–95	661.35	125.20	141.10	129.75
1995–96	744.16	112.52	137.18	126.15
1996–97	539.33	72.47	165.18	151.90
1997–98	401.34	74.41	197.20	181.35

Source : Office of the Assistant Directorate of Textiles, Orissa, Berhampur.

From Table 12.4, it is evident that the sales have increased at best continuously upto the year 1995-96 and there after it has fallen suddenly and cumulative unsold stock have increased continuously which may be treated as a big threat towards the long-term viability of PHWCSs.

As PHWCSs are certainly the associations for the sake of the business of its members, if it suffers from accumulative stock, it may retard the growth potentials of handloom industry. It is expected that in the long run it will hamper the employment of the wage rate of the member weavers. In Table 12.5, an attempt has been made to calculate the degree of correlation between employment and cumulative unsold stock. Further Fig. 12.2 explains the sales index histogram.

From Table 12.5, correlation (r) between employment and unsold stock is found to be greater than 0 and less than 1 i.e. $0 < r < 1$. This shows that the unsold cumulative stock does not retard weavers from this industry. May it be stated that as it is their profession by inheritance,

Table 12.5 : Correlation between the Unsold Items of PHWCSs and the Level of Employment in the PHWCSs

Years	*Employment (X)	X $(x-\bar{x})$	**Unsold items (in lakhs) Y	Y $(Y-\bar{Y})$	X^2	Y^2	XY
1990–91	8201	–13.25	108.74	–39.37	175.56	1549.99	521.65
1991–92	7202	–1017.25	113.77	–34.37	1034797.5	1181.29	34932.36
1992–93	8350	130.75	125.81	–22.3	17095.56	497.29	–2915.72
1993–94	8544	324.75	195.35	77.24	105462.56	2231.61	15341.19
1994–95	8460	240.75	141.10	–70.1	57960.56	7914.01	–16876.57
1995–96	8598	375.75	137.18	–10.93	141188.06	119.46	–4106.94
1996–97	8442	222.75	165.80	17.69	49617.56	312.93	3940.44
1197–98	7952	–267.25	197.20	49.09	71422.56	2409.82	–13119.30
	ΣX = 65754		ΣY= 1184.95		ΣX^2 = 1477719.5	ΣY^2 = 13214.4	ΣXY = 22322.11

Source : * and ** Additional Directorate of Textiles, Berhampur, Ganjam, Orissa.

$$\bar{X}=\frac{\Sigma X}{N}=\frac{65.754}{8}=8219.25;$$

$$\bar{Y}=\frac{\Sigma Y}{N}=\frac{1184.95}{8}=148.11$$

$$r=\frac{\Sigma XY}{\sqrt{\Sigma X^2.\Sigma Y^2}}=\frac{22322.11}{\sqrt{147719.5\times 13214.4}}=0.50>0$$

therefore, easily the weavers cannot leave the industry. Rather, despite hardships, they struggle within the industry.

Price Index

To show the price change for the products produced by the PHWCSs, Price Index Number has been calculated by employing Durbish and Bowley's Method. Table 12.6 illustrates the preparation of price index.

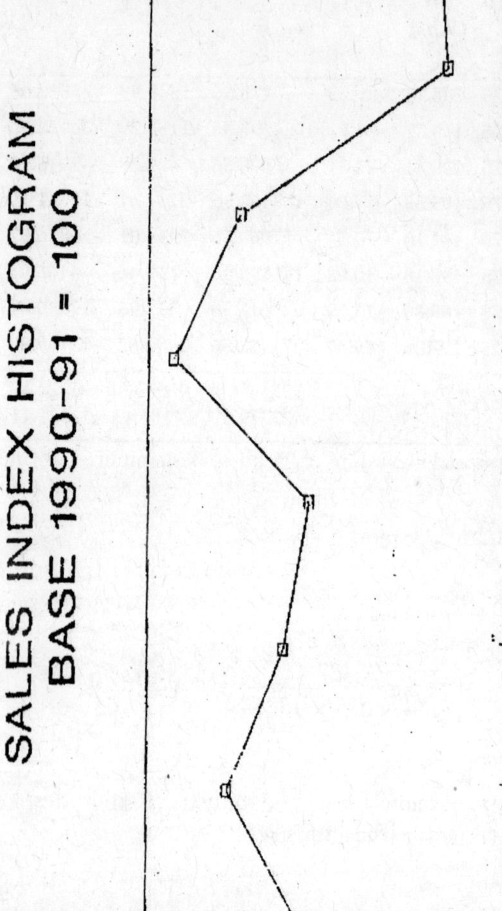

Fig. 12.2 : Sales Index Histogram (Base 1990–91 =100)

Dorbish and Bowley's Price Index

$$P_{01} = \frac{L+P}{2}$$

where

L = Laspeyer's Index

P = Pasche's Index

$$P_{01} = \frac{\dfrac{\Sigma p_1 q_0}{\Sigma p_0 q_0} + \dfrac{\Sigma p_1 q_1}{\Sigma p_0 q_0}}{2} \times 100$$

$$= \frac{\dfrac{855359.92}{453547.63} + \dfrac{461356.93}{453547.67}}{2} \times 100$$

$$= 145.1$$

Thus, the price level for the range of the products produced by PHWCSs has increased by 45.1 percent.

Table 12.6 : Price Index

Items	*Average price in* 1990-91 p_0	*Average quantity* sold in 1990-91 q_0	*Average price in* 1997-98 p_1	*Average quantity* sold in 1997-98 q_1	p_0q_0	p_1q_0	p_1q_1
Towel (Y-2)	12.48	332	32.80	589	4143.36	12529.6	19319.2
Dhoti (Y-26)	27.73	1500	48.64	623	41595.00	72960.0	30302.7
Dhoti (Y-26)	43.70	500	81.75	959	21850.00	40975.0	78590.05
Saree (Y-40)	80.75	226	102.07	679	18249.50	23067.8	69305.53
Saree Y-26)	40.51	9077	77.76	3393	367709.27	705827.52	263839.65
Total					Σp_0q_0 = 453547.63	Σp_1q_0 = 855359.92	Σp_1q_1 = 461356.93

Source : Compiled from the Annual Audit Reports of G. Damodarpalli and Mundamarai

Table 12.7 : Materials Cost Index

Components of cost	Average cost per PHWCS 1990–91 (in Rs.) p_0	Average cost per PHWCS 1997–98 (in Rs.) p_1
Wage	1,63,238.00	1,69,636.30
Yarn	4,23,336.00	3,89,138.85
Training for labour	5,000.00	7,000.00
	Σp_0 = 591574.00	Σp_1 = 565775.05

Materials Cost Index by Simple Aggregate Method :

$$P_{01} = \frac{\Sigma p_1}{\Sigma p_0} \times 100$$

$$= \frac{56775.00}{591574.05} \times 100$$

$$= 95.6$$

Materials Cost Index

To examine the changes in the cost conditions, materials cost has been calculated and Table 12.7 prepares the Materials Cost Index.

This means that as compared to 1990-91 costs, there is a net decrease in the materials cost of PHWCSs, to the extent of 100–95.6 = 4.4 percent.

As price index increases by 45.1 percent and materials cost decreases by 4.4 percent, therefore, it is not the relevant trace of intelligence on the part of PHWCSs to enhance the price level for maximizing profit.

Findings of the Study

On the basis of the different parameters studied in this paper, following findings have emerged :

1. At the beginning of the study period, there were 68 PHWCSs in Ganjam district and their numbers decreased to 65 in the year 1993-94, which continues till date. This means, 23 PHWCSs have become domant in recent years (Table 12.1).

2. The percentage share of the profit making PHWCSs gradually declines from 94.11 percent in the year 1990-91 to 78.46 percent in the year 1997-98. The percentage share of loss making and no-profit/no-loss making PHWCSs increase. (Table 12.1).
3. The total production of PHWCSs falls by 21.2 percent in the year 1997-98 in comparison to the year 1990-91. But over the entire study period, production has increased marginally which is evident from the Fig. 12.1 (Table 12.2).
4. Barring the years 1992-92 and 1994-95, the total sales of PHWCSs have fallen during all the years under study (Fig. 12.2).
5. A secularly increasing trend is found in the cumulative stock of PHWCSs. The commutative stock Index for the year 1997-98 stands at 181.35 in comparison to the 100 in the year 1990–91. Perhaps it is the most serious problem encounters by the PHWCSs (Table 12.5).
6. The degree of correlation between cumulative stock and employment is found positive which implies cumulative stock of PHWCSs' doesn't hamper significantly the quantum of employment (Table 12.5).
7. There appears an increasing price index and decreasing Materials cost index (Table 12.6 and Table 12.7).

The viability of PHWCSs remains with their growth in terms of the number of PHWCSs, total production & total sales. But, unfortunately accumulated unsold stock of clothes constitute a serious menace on the path of the progress of PHWCSs.

It is hightime for the PHWCSs to be indulged in better selling strategies. As the price rise of 45.1 percent for their products is sufficiently attractive, therefore, to dispose of the unsold stock, clearance sales should be undertaken immediately. The merchandise of final goods so produced by PHWCSs must not be confined to the selling counters of the society. The products must be well advertised. There should be the budgetary provision of selling outlay in the respective budgets of PHWCSs. Majority of the PHWCSs don't introduce labeling, proper packing and nevertheless extend sufficient attention towards colour, design, quality (R.K.Panda). Thus, it is the best time for them to pay suitable attention towards advertisement. product-mix, labeling, packaging suitable colour, design etc. so that they can come out of best success in the field of marketing. Twenty first century definitely encounters the problem of marketing. If the different personnel, Weavers and the ministry of textiles adopt strong marketing strategies, the problems of PHWCSs can be mitigated, no doubt.

Hence, it may be suggested that the provision of adequate finance, procurement of quality raw materials, implementation of new technology, education for better skill formation to the weavers, sincerity of the employees of directorate and Asst. directorate of Textiles, better selling strategies etc. can go a long way in combating the phenomenal problems of PHWCSs. Though profit is not the motive of a co-operative organisation, still PHWCSs have to earn profit to maintain the weavers in a lucrative stand.

References

1. Jyoti Rani, T & Prema Kumari, C.H. (1998), Impact and evaluation of Cotton-Silk Handloom Weaver's Co-operative Societies. A study in rural Area, Kuruskhetra, February, 1998, Vol. XLVI, NO.-5.
2. Economic Survey [1997-98], Government of India, P-108.
3. The Hindu Survey of Indian Industry (1996), P-369.
4. Orissa Handloom Basic Facts (1997), Directorate of Textiles, Orissa, Bhubaneswar.
5. Annual Report, 1997-98, Directorate of Textiles, Orissa, Bhubaneswar.
6. Orissa Handloom Basic Facts (1997) opcit.
7. Panda, Radhakrushna (1998); "Problems and prospects of Primary Handloom Weavers' Co-operative Societies in Orissa in S.N. Tripathy (Ed.), Co-operatives, for rural Development, Discovery Publishing House, New Delhi, pp. 162.163.

13

Socio-Economic Status of Co-operative Handloom Weavers

A Case Study

Dr. (Mrs.) Punithavathy Pandian*

M.A., M.Com., M.Phil. Ph.D.

and Ms. J. Jansi Rani**

M.Com., M.Phil.

Handloom Industry is considered to be a major economic activity in Tamil Nadu. There are many cities and towns which are popular for manufacturing of or more handloom products in Tamil Nadu. Places like Pallipalayam, Aruppukottai, Kancheepuram, Salem, Sithyenkottai, Chinnalapatti, Trichy, Kangeyam and Madurai are known for different varieties of handloom products.

The handloom industry in Tamil Nadu can be classified into three groups, viz., the co-operatives, the master weavers and independent weavers.The role played by the Co-operatives can be attributed as a major cause towards the growth of handloom industry in Tamil Nadu with Co-operative handloom weavers societies at village level and the state level playing a significant role in the development of handloom in production, marketing and exports. One of the important products manufactured under the handloom sector is an art - silk sarees. Though they are considered second to pure silk they have been recognised as poor woman's engagement saree. It being an imitation of pure silk is called so because the products do not have purity in quality and are inferior to pure silk.

* Dr. (Mrs.) Pandian is the Professor or Commerce, Madurai—Kamraj University, Madhurai—625 021.

**Ms. Jansi Rani is a researcher.

The different places in Tamil Nadu where the art-silk sarees manufactured are Aruppukottai, Chinnalapatti, Madurai and Salem. Manufacture of Art silk saree is the primary occupation of a large number of poor people in the above mentioned places. The Government also provides help to the co-operative society by giving financial, marketing and technical support. It is witnessed, that only few of the industrial weavers co-operatives societies earn profit inspite of the patronage given by the Government. The performance of the society is closely linked with the weavers performance. And, it is necessary to analyse the weavers' standard of living which largely contributes to their performance. The Co-operative societies are mainly formulated for the uplifement of the living standards of the hand-loom weavers. Hence, the socio-economic conditions of the weavers also have to be analysed.

Data

Primary data regarding in the socio-economic status of handloom weavers in the co-operative society are collected through structured schedule in Aruppukottai Town, Tamil Nadu in the year 1994. Hundred households were selected for the study purpose. The selected weavers mainly weave art silk sarees.

Age and Sex-wise Composition of Weavers

Handloom weaving needs lot of skill and physical strength. Age and Sex composition influence the productive capacity of the weavers. The age and sex composition of the weavers are given below in Table 13.1.

Table 13.1 : Age and Sex-wise Composition

Age Group	*Male*	*Female*	*Total*
18 – 20	2	15	17
21 – 30	5	25	30
31 – 40	7	30	37
41 – 50	4	10	14
Above 50	0	2	2

Analysis of the sex-wise composition of the weavers shows that 82 per cent of the weavers belong to fair sex. In most of the cases weaving has been done by the female members of the family to supplement the income of the household. Another convenience in this occupation is female members can stay at home and earn money. Working hours can be altered to their convenience. Fifty five per cent of the weavers are in the age group of 21 to 40. This is the period one can experience robust health and weaving can be done more efficiently. The number of weavers above the age 50 is very meagre.

Educational Status of the Weavers

Education yields huge set of benefits to the individual concerned and to the society in the form of larger set of externalities. The educational status of the weavers are given in the Table 13.2.

Table 13.2 : Educational Status of the Weavers

Category	*Male*	*Female*	*Total*
Illiterate	3	33	36
Elementary	7	13	20
S.S.L.C.	4	23	27
H.S.C.	3	11	14
Graduate	1	2	3

The above Table 13.2 gives educational status of the weavers. About 36 per cent of the weavers are illiterates. Education was deprived to these weaves due to poverty and working since childhood.

Family Size

There exists a close relationship between the size of the household and standard of living of the household.

Table 13.3 : The Average Household Size

Household Income Group	*No. of Households*	*No. of Persons*	*Average Household Size*
Upto 1000	23	106	4.7
1000 – 1500	33	211	5.0
1500 – 2000	25	131	3.7
2000 – 2500	11	80	3.8
2500 – 3000	8	51	4.4

The above Table 13.3 shows the average size of the households in each household income group. There are some minor fluctuations in the household size of the various income groups. In general the average size of the households shows a declining trend over the increase in the income groups. The lowest income group has an average household size of 4.7 members and the highest income group has a size of 4.4 members. Another and even more useful way of finding out the severity of the household size affecting the standard of living of the people can be done by computing the dependency ratio. The dependency ratio is based on the fact that every member of the society is a consumer while some are producers. A household with a larger proportion of its members producing goods and services is economically better off than a household with a smaller proportion of producers.

The Table 13.4 shows the dependency ratio of different income groups. The dependency ratio like the household size, decreases with the increase in income groups except for the Rs. 1000 – 1500 income group. The lowest income group has the dependency ratio of 1.81 and the highest income group the lowest dependency ratio of 1.31.

Table 13.4 : Dependency Ratio

Household Income Group	*Dependents*	*Earning Persons*	*Ratio*
Upto 1000	40	27	1 : 1.81
1000 – 1500	99	37	1 : 2.68
1500 – 2000	59	32	1 : 1.84
2000 – 2500	50	27	1 : 1.85
2500 – 3000	21	16	1 : 1.31

Income is the parameter to measure the standard of living of the people to ascertain the financial potentiality of the people. Income of the weaves are given in Table 13.5.

Table 13.5 : Sources of Average Household Monthly Income

Income Groups	*No. of House-holds*	*Average Monthly Income per Household*	
		Weaving	*Other Occupation*
Upto 1000	23	475	515
1000 – 1500	33	385	1,020
1500 – 2000	25	630	1,260
2000 – 2500	11	540	1,770
2500 – 3000	8	321	2,450

Most of the family members in the weaving community is engaged in other occupation than weaving. The lowest income group mainly depends on weaving. But, the highest income group earns comparatively lesser amount from weaving.

To find out the degree of inequality in the income distribution among the sample respondents Gini ratio has been calculated on the basis of the following formula:

$$L = 1 - \frac{\sum_{K=1}^{N} (P_K - P_{K-1})(Q_K + Q_{K-1})}{10,000}$$

where L = Gini Ratio

P_K = Cumulative Percentage of Persons

Q_K = Cumulative Percentage of Income

N = Number of Classes used in the Analysis

The value of Gini Ratio (L) can range from 0 to 1. Computation Gini Ratio on the basis of the above formula is given in the following Table 13.6.

Table 13.6 : Calculation of Gini Ratio

Frequency (Household)	*Cumulative Frequency Household* P_K	*Total Income*	*Cumulative Income*	*Cumulative Income Percentage* Q_K
23	23	11,500	11,500	8
33	.56	41,250	52,750	36.8
25	81	43,750	96,500	67.4
11	92	24,750	1,21,250	84.6
8	100	22,000	1,43,250	100

$$L = 1 - \frac{7,416.2}{10,000} = .74$$

$$= 1 - .74 = .26$$

The obtained Gini Ratio value of 0.26 leads to the inference that there is income inequality in the distribution of income among the sample weavers. This income inequality may be due to the fact that in the higher income group weaving is a subsidiary occupation.

Wages

Wages can be defined as the remuneration paid by the employer for the services of a worker. Wages in the widest sense mean any economic compensation paid to the working people by the employer under some contract for the services rendered by them. 'A' class skilled labourers are needed for weaving are silk sarees.

Labourers are paid wages on the basis of the number of pieces they make. The piece wage rates are calculated on the basis of work done. A person with more efficiency receives more wages.

Table 13.7 : Wage Structure

(in Rs.)

Years	*Putta Saree*	*Marippu Saree*	*Marippu+ Putta Saree*
1983–84	13.25	12.85	24.50
1984–85	13.35	12.85	24.50
1985–86	14.75	14.35	26.00
1986–87	14.75	14.35	26.00
1987–88	14.75	14.35	26.00
1988–89	14.75	14.35	26.00
1989–90	16.20	15.75	27.50
1990–91	18.00	17.35	28.80
1991–92	18.00	17.35	28.00
1992–93	21.65	20.85	30.45

The wage rate has remained constant from 1985 to 1989. Then the wage rate has experienced a mild increase over the years, compared to increase in the price of raw materials, the wage rate has increased moderately only. Present wage rate in 1994; Putta Saree is rupees 23.80, Marippu Saree is rupees 22.95 and Marippu Plus Putta Saree is rupees 33.50.

Analysis of Expenditure

The levels of living of the people is judged by the levels of per capita expenditure. Properly speaking, the level of living has two components primary and secondary. The primary components of living include nutrition, housing, medical care, clothing and education. The secondary components leisure, security and the environment. The expenditure on primary components by an average household an be treated as an approximate indicator of the level of living.

Household expenditure in this study means the total expenditure on the household items like food, fuel, clothing, education and other items. Per capita expenditure of each income class has been tabulated and presented in Table 13.8.

Table 13.8 : Per Capita Monthly Expenditure

Income Group	*House-hold Size*	*Food*		*Non-Food Item*	
		Amount	*Percentage*	*Amount*	*Percentage*
Upto 1000	4.7	163.2	74.2	56.8	25.8
1000–1500	5.0	212.5	71.3	85.5	28.7
1500–2000	3.7	314.2	69.5	137.8	30.5
2000–2500	3.8	440.2	67.2	214.8	32.8
2500–3000	4.4	445.2	64.9	240.8	35.1

In accordance with the survey estimate, the per capita monthly expenditure of the low income group is Rs. 210/- and of the highest expenditure group is Rs. 686/-. The disparity in private consumption expenditure of the low income group is also revealed in Table 13.9.

Table 13.9 : Consumption of Food Items

Income Group	*Milk (%age)*	*Meat & Egg (%age)*	*Vege-tables (%age)*	*Food-grain and other Cereals (%age)*
Upto 1000	1.8	2.8	7.7	61.9
1000–1500	3.5	3.9	8.2	56.7
1500–2000	4.2	6.2	7.4	51.7
2000–2500	5.6	8.3	9.8	43.5
2500–3000	7.3	11.6	10.5	35.5

Note : Percentage of each item is worked out of total expenditure.

In this connection, it may be useful to explain certain concepts. One is Engel's law of consumption. According to this, at very low level of income, a major proportion of income is spent on food products and a very small proportion on non-food items such as entertainment, travels, education and health.

Secondly, as has been explained by Zimmerman, with the rise in income from a low level, a large part of the income gets used up for food products and other necessaries. In other words, when the income of the poor rises, they spend more to get better food. It is only after having reached a certain minimum standard of living that people go in for other goods.

Thirdly, according to Colin Clark, economic development and a rising standard of living can be said to have taken place, when the proportion of expenditure on consumption and necessities declines and that on other goods increases. A change in the pattern of expenditure on consumption is an index of economic development and improvement of economic life.

The applicability of the above statements can very well be seen here. The study shows the fact that a lion's share of the income is spent on food but only a negligible amount is set apart for clothing and shelter. As and when income increase, expenditure on food items also shoots up in the initial stage. However, there are some checks and balance with regard to additional income which come into their pockets.

The proportion of expenditure devoted to food decreases steadily with the increase in income and expenditure. In the lower income groups, 74.2 per cent of the total expenditure is for food items alone. The proportion slowly decreases with every successive increase in income even though it shows a minor fluctuation between the various income groups. Those with the highest per capita expenditure devoted only about 64.9 per cent of their total expenditure to food items. Comparative analysis indicates that the proportion of expenditure allotted for food is substantially lesser for the high income group and higher for the low income group. If the percentage of consumption on items other than food is to be viewed as a criteria for measuring the standard of living of the community, the standard of living of the weavers in the low income group can be identified as poor.

Consumption Pattern

Foodgrains include cereals, cereal substitutes and pulses. Rice is the main cereal. Food grains account for a full two thirds of expenditure on food with little being spent on items of 'other goods' like milk, meat etc., which are necessary components, besides food grains, for a balanced and nutritious diet.

In case of majority of population in the surveyed household cereals form almost a bulk of the diet and constitute a major source. If not the only source of nutrients particularly in the case of people belonging to lower economic groups. This is evident from the data furnished in Table 13.9 where in one can perceive with the money value spent on food grains by the lower expenditure group is high. Also is understood from the study that the money spent on food grains steadily declines and the percentage of money spent on others steadily increases.

In this study the lowest income group households spent a bare minimum amount of 1.6 per cent for consumption of milk and milk products. But highest income group of the weavers spent 7.3 per cent of the food expenditure.

The lowest income group people nearly 2.8 per cent on their fish, egg and meat. On festival occasion they incurs expenditure to buy bulk quality of meat and other extra items.

Vegetables claim a larger percentage next to the foodgrains. A comparative analysis of consumption of meat, fish and egg and vegetable reveals that the low income group spend a higher percentage on vegetables i.e. 7.6 per cent which comes next to the cereals and food grains. This clearly indicates that in the higher income brackets more money is spent on meat, fish and egg than on the vegetables resulting in protein sufficiency. The other food items includes grams, edible oils, salt and species. The consumption rate is much high in higher income groups when compared to the lower income groups.

Consumption Pattern of Non-food Items

A comparative analysis of per capita cloth consumption expenditure figures throws light on the inequality that prevails between the income groups. The Table 13.10 shows the average per capita expenditure by the low income and the highest income households. The

Table 13.10 : Per Capita Expenditure Pattern of Non-Food Items in the Total Expenditure

Income Group	*Cloth %age*	*Medicine %age*	*Education %age*	*Miscellaneous %age*
Upto 1000	13.7	3.9	0.65	7.5
1000–1500	16.2	2.7	1.40	8.4
1500–2000	14.8	2.9	2.70	10.1
2000–2500	15.6	3.2	4.69	9.4
2500–3000	17.7	4.8	2.90	9.7

Note : Percentage of each item is worked out of total expenditure.

lowest income group in the survey has a lowest average per capita cloth consumption than the highest group.

Apart from the per capita consumer expenditure on other items viz., expenditure on education, fuel, lighting and other miscellaneous items is higher in the case of high income households. The money spent on medicine registered a steady improvement. Only a little attention is paid for medicine and this is mainly due to low income availability. Most of the lower income group households report to local medicine and if they do not get cured, they try to make use of the free medical facility provided by Government Hospital.

Of all the categorised items, only a microscopic amount is spent on education which consists only lower per cent of the total expenditure. The low income group spends a very low amount for educating their children.

finally, the miscellaneous items include the expenditure on travel, cosmetics, tobacco entertainment, footwear and washing. The expenditure also shows a steady increase from the lower income to the higher income group.

Occupational Diseases

By nature of their profession of the weavers and persons engaged in the ancillary industries are specially liable to fell a prey to a diseases like asthma, cough, tuberculosis and anemia. Their eye sight is also affected due to eye strain in weaving. One third of the sample respondents suffer from asthma.

Analysis of Debt

The analysis of debt reveals the economic backwardness of the weavers.

Table 13.11 : Debt Groups of Sample Weavers

Debt Groups	*No. of Respondents*
Below 1,000	46
1,000–5,000	12
5,000–10,000	5
10,000–20,000	3
No Debt	34

Accordingly to Table 13.11, only 34 sample weavers are free from debt: 46 respondents have debt upto Rs. 1,000/-. The analysis reveals that majority of the respondents are indebted.

The different sources of debt of the respondents are given in Table 13.12.

Table 13.12 : Sources of Debt

Sources	*No. of Respondents*
Local Money Lender	48
Friends and Relatives	12
Banks	6
Free from Debt	34

The above Table 13.12 reveals that the major sources of debt is the local money lender. The abnormal rate of interest charged by the money lenders has become a permanent burden for the weavers.

Reasons for Indebtedness

Reason for the indebtedness of the respondents are investigated and presented in Table 13.13.

Table 13.13 : Reason for Indebtedness

Reasons	*No. of Respondents*
Households Expenditure	32
Festival and Ceremonies	13
Medical Expenditure	12
Marriage	9

It is clear that majority borrowings are for the household expenditure. Twelve per cent borrow for medical purpose and 12 per cent borrow for festival ceremonies. This shows the weavers inability to meet their day-to-day expenses.

Conclusion

Weaving is the main occupation for the lowest income group. It becomes a subsidiary occupation for the highest income group. Sex composition of the weavers showed a bias towards fair sex. With the increase in income more money is spent for nutrients like milk, meat and egg. Weavers mainly get loans from money lenders. Therefore, co-operatives should be organised in a big way to provide financial needs of the weavers.

14

Marketing of Handloom Fabrics by Co-optex in Tamil Nadu

*Dr. V. Rangaswamy**
*Dr. J. Jabarullahan***

The handloom industry is one of the largest cottage industries and it occupies a place of prominence in the economy in India. It is estimated that the handloom industry produces nearly one-third of the country's requirements of cloth. Although the handloom industry is spread all over India, it is concentrated mainly in Tamil nadu, Andhra Pradesh, Uttar Pradesh, West Bengal, Rajasthan, Orissa, Karnataka, Bihar, Tripura, Kerala and Maharashtra. Among the various handloom cloth-producting states in India, Tamil Nadu occupies an important place and the handloom silk sarees of Kancheepuram has a worldwide market. In Tamil Nadu during 1993, there were 1410 primarily weavers co-operative societies with 3.79 lakh weavers as members, amounting to 88 per cent coming under co-operatives. In this article an attempt has been made to analyse the marketing of handlooms by the Tamil Nadu Handloom Weavers co-operative Society Limited, popularly known as "co-optex".

Role of Handloom Co-operatives

Handloom weavers are self-employed cottage industry workers. They are poor, illiterate, disorganised and spread over in rural areas. They do not get employment throughout the year, due to non-availability of yarn produced by the mills. The price of yarn fluctuates very often and the poor weavers face the problem of marketing their finished fabrics. They find it also difficult to solve their financial

* Professor, Department of Commerce, Madurai, Kamraj University, Madurai—625 021.
**Head of the Department of Commerce, Sri S. R. Naidu Memorial College, Sathur (Tamil Nadu).

problems. Hence, they are forced to work under the master weavers for low wages. Weavers borrow from the master weaver to satisfy their family needs. But, they find it difficult to repay the loans borrowed from the master weaver and are forced to work as bonded labourers. In order to solve such problems, the Government of India announced a policy to promote the handloom industry by organizing weavers' co-operative societies. For the past four decades the State and the Central Governments have been taking steps to bring all the handloom weavers in India under the co-operative fold.

Weavers' co-operative societies in Tamil Nadu include separate societies for cotton and silk fabrics. Societies for Cotton handloom goods are formed in places where cotton goods are produced in plenty. The Silk Handloom Weavers Co-operative Societies function mainly in places like Kancheepuram, Arani, Kumbakonam, and Salem. Co-optex has been formed by the Government of Tamil Nadu as an apex agency to provide financial and marketing assistance to all the handloom weavers' of co-operative societies in the State.

Structure of Weavers' Co-operative Societies in India

The Four-tier structure of handloom weavers, co-operative societies in India is shown in Figure 14.1.

Structure of Weavers' Co-operative Societies in India

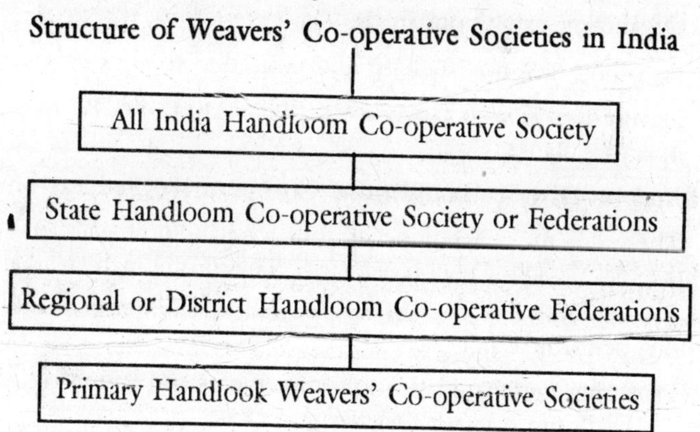

All India Handloom Fabrics Marketing Co-operative Society

All India Handloom Fabrics Marketing Co-operative Society functions at the National level. All India Handloom Fabrics Marketing Co-operative Society acts as an apex body for all the State Handloom Co-operative Societies or Federations functioning at state level in various

States in India. The important functions of the All India Handloom Fabrics Marketing Co-operative Society are:

1. Promoting domestic and export market for handloom fabrics produced by primary handloom co-operative societies.
2. Arranging for the sale of handloom fabrics.
3. Conducting exhibitions.
4. Publishing market information on handloom fabrics and
5. Having liaison with Government of India, NCDC, NABARD, All India Handloom Board and Co-operative Institutions.

State Handloom Co-operative Society/Federation

This organisation acts as an apex body for the handloom weaver's co-operative societies functioning in the respective States. It promotes the marketing of handloom fabrics produced by member societies in the state. All the Regional or District Handloom Co-operative Federations are the members of this society. The important functions of the State Handloom Co-operative Society/Federation are:

1. Procuring raw materials, tools and supplying to member societies.
2. Marketing of finished goods of member societies.
3. Organizing exhibitions in the State.
4. Providing technical training and education to weavers and
5. Having liaison with Government, NABARD, NCDC and Co-operative Banks.

Regional or District Handloom Co-operative Federations

These are the federations of primary handloom weavers' co-operative societies in the region or district. They promote the marketing of handloom fabrics in the regional or district levels. The important functions performed are:

1. Procuring raw materials, tools implements and supplying them to handloom primary societies and
2. The marketing of finished goods of primary societies.

Primary Handloom Weaver's Co-operative Societies

These are the actual units which produce handloom fabrics. The important cautions of primary handloom weavers' co-operative societies are:

1. Raising funds from different sources including member weavers and Government.
2. Procuring raw materials, tools implements and supply them to weaver members.
3. Collecting the finished goods from weaver members and marketing them to serve the interest of the member weavers and societies.

Marketing in Handloom Industry

The greatest problem of the handloom industry has been the marketing of finished cloth. It has to face the stiff competition from the well-organised and mechanised mill sector. The handloom cloth suffers from inherent defects such as lack of uniformity in texture, dimensions and finish. The fading of colours and shrinkage are usual complaints made against handloom fabrics. Lack of standardisation in quality has generated an apathy in the consumers and has driven them towards mill-made fabrics. The marketable capacity and market potentials are the important factors that decide the success of handloom co-operative societies. More often than not, the weavers' co-operative societies face accumulated unsold stocks.

Role of Co-Optex

The Tamil Nadu Handloom Weavers' Co-operative Society Limited popularly known as Co-optex, was started on August 12, 1935, to co-ordinate and harness the activities of primary handloom weavers and the co-operative societies in Madras Province.

Objects of Co-optex

The main objects of the Co-optex are:

i) To arrange for the purchase of the raw material and appliances required for the primary handloom weavers' co-operative societies in Tamil Nadu.

ii) To procure the finished products of affiliated primary weaver's co-operative societies and arrange for their sale of the best advantage of Co-optex and member co-optex societies.

iii) To provide financial and managerial help to the primary handloom weavers' co-operative societies and

iv) To advise the affiliated societies to produce improved and easily marketable varieties of handloom fabrics.

The management of Co-optex has been organised on functional lines. The major functions are finance, procurement, marketing, personnel, export and product development. Each function is headed by a manager. Co-optex is under the control of the Director of Handlooms and Textiles, who is incharge of the development of handloom industry in Tamil Nadu.

The Directorate of Handloom allots yarn to Co-optex to be distributed to the Primary Handloom Weavers' co-operative societies. The procurement and marketing of handloom goods are the main activities of Co-optex. The fabrics procured and sold by Co-optex are of the following varieties:

I. Silk Fabrics

a) Sarees
b) Dhoties
c) Shirtings
d) Angavasthirams

II. Cotton Fabrics

a) Sarees
b) Dhoties
c) Shirtings
d) Suitings
e) Bed Sheets
f) Furnishings
h) Jammakkalam
i) Lungies
j) Towels
k) Pillow covers

III. Polyester Fabrics

a) Sarees
b) Dhoties
c) Shirtings
d) Suitings

IV. **Janatha Varieties**

a) Sarees

b) Dhoties and

c) Colour Gada

For the purpose of procurement, the State of Tamil Nadu has been divided into 11 regions. Table 14.1 presents the details of the area covered for each region.

Table 14.1 : Details of Regional Procurement Centres of Co-optex

Sl. No.	*Regions*	*Jurisdiction*
1.	Coimbatore	Coimbatore and Nilgris districts
2.	Cuddalore	South Arcot, Thanjavure and Nagai Quaid–E.Milleth Districts.
3.	Erode	Periyar District
4.	Kanchipuram (Silk)	Kancheepuram and Arani Area Silk Societies
5.	Madurai I	Kamarajar, Pasumpon, Muthuramainga Thevar Districts.
6.	Madurai II	Anna, Ramnad and Madurai Districts.
7.	Trichy	Trichy and Pudukottai
8.	Salem	Salem and Dharampuri Districts.
9.	Tirunelveli	V.O. Chidambaranar, Nellai Kattabomman and Kanyakumari Districits.
10.	Vellore	Madras, Chengai M.G.R., Thiruvanamali Sambuvarayar, North Arcot Ambedkar Districts.
11.	Contract Production at Erode	Government supply and Tamil Nadu Co operative Textile Processing Mills.

Source : Compiled from the Unpublished Records of Co-optex

The various varieties of fabrics procured by Co-optex can be grouped under the following types :

1. Polyster
2. Janatha Variety
3. Silk
4. Cotton Variety and

5. Others.

Table 14.2 shows the variety-wise procurement by Co-optex during the 11 years from 1983–84 to 1993–94.

Channels of Distribution

The handloom co-operatives produce fabrics meant for consumers but they are routed through four alternative channels. They are:

1. Handloom Co-operatives-wholesalers-Retailers-consumers.
2. Handloom Co-operatives-Co-optex-Consumers.
3. Handloom Co-operatives-Retailers-Consumers and
4. Handloom Co-operatives-Consumers.

Among the four alternative channels available for the sale of handloom fabrics, the main channel is Co-optex. In this regard, Co-optex functions as a wholesaler. Co-optex acts as a link between the fabrics producing co-operative society and the ultimate consumer. It stocks large quantities of handloom fabrics in its 11 regional warehouses situated at Coimbatore, Cuddalore, Erode, Kanchipuram, Madurai, Trichy, Salem, Tiruneveli and Vellore.

Co-optex sells the handloom fabrics procured from the primaries through its 423 retails outlets. It procures the fabrics from primary handloom weavers co-operative societies in large quantities based on the demand made by the retails outlets. After the procurement they are segregated product-wise like sarees, dhoties, towels, bed-sheets, pillow covers and the like. They are also classified both according to their quality and yarn counts. Before the fabrics are sent to the retail outlets, the Co-optex affixes its emblem and the price labels on the fabrics.

The co-optex has the dual functions of wholesaling and retailing of handloom fabrics. As a wholesaler of handloom fabrics, the Co-optex pursues the marketing activities such as storing, grading and labelling of fabrics. The head office of Co-optex at Madras does not make any direct sales. The head office acts only as a co-ordinator for the procurement of handloom fabrics from primaries and sells through its retail outlets. The 11 regional offices of Co-optex also do not make any direct sales to the consumers.

The retails outlets of Co-optex occupy a key position in the channel of marketing by virtue of their direct contact with the consumers. The retail outlets are the last link or intermediary between the co-optex and

Table 14.2 : Variety-wise Procurement of Fabrics by Co-optex

(Rupees in Lakhs)

Year	Polyster (Rs.)	Janatha (Rs.)	Silk (Rs.)	Cotton (Rs.)	Others (Rs.)	Total (Rs.)
1983–84	1199.00 (16.94)	1558.00 (22.01	476.00 (6.72)	1099.00 (15.53)	2747.00 (38.80)	7079.00 (100)
1984–85	1198.96 (20.05)	1557.77 (26.05)	476.23 (7.96)	269.10 (4.50)	2478.18 (41.44)	5980.24 (100)
1985–86	1195.35 (16.83)	1994.16 (28.08)	738.32 (10.40)	369.05 (5.20)	2803.74 (39.49)	7100.62 (100)
1986–87	1125.53 (17.24)	1421.86 (21.78)	684.72 (10.49)	526.97 (8.07)	2768.76 (42.42)	6527.84 (100)
1987–88	794.83 (14.00)	1494.52 (26.33)	930.03 (16.38)	151.41 (2.67)	2306.32 (40.62)	5677.11 (100)
1988–89	837.86 (11.55)	1418.64 (19.56)	1726.70 (23.80)	499.92 (6.89)	2771.10 (38.20)	7254.22 (100)
1989–90	530.19 (5.75)	4366.04 (47.38)	1370.63 (14.87)	206.55 (2.25)	2741.08 (29.75)	9214.49 (100)
1990–91	910.98 (9.59)	2232.02 (23.49)	2032.50 (21.39)	495.48 (5.21)	3832.26 (40.32)	9503.24 (100)
1991–92	1652.70 (12.66)	2191.69 (16.79)	3961.05 (30.35)	723.38 (5.54)	4524.18 (34.66)	13053.00 (100)
1992–93	920.58 (7.21)	3451.92 (27.02)	3286.17 (25.72)	1127.11 (8.82)	3990.22 (31.23)	12776.00 (100)
1993–94	1022.27 (8.68)	2370.25 (20.12)	2409.97 (20.45)	1767.84 (15.00)	4211.75 (35.75)	11782.08 (100)

Source : Co-optex Production Department Records—Madras.

Note : Figures in parenthesis indicate percentage to total.

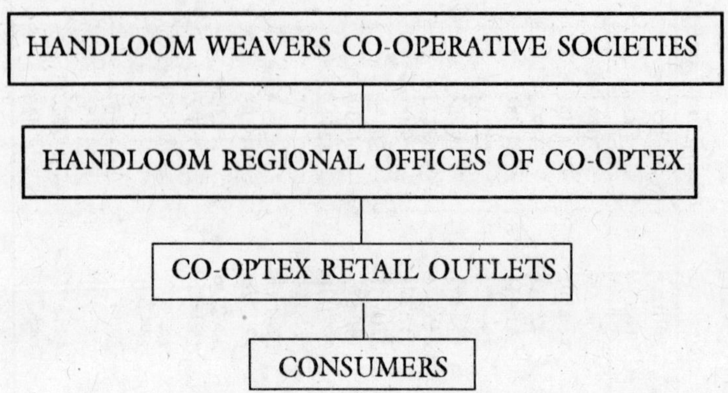

Fig. 14.2 : Channels of Distribution for Handloom Fabrics

the ultimate consumers. Figure 14.2 shows the channels through which the handloom fabrics of the primary societies reach the consumer.

Table 14.3 shows the sales performance of Co-optex retail outlets.

Table 14.3 : Sales Performance of Co-optex Retail Outlets

Sl. No.	*Year*	*No. of Retail Outlets*	*Sales made (Rs. in Lakhs)*	*Average Sales per Retail Outlets (Rs. in Lakhs)* (4) ÷ (3)
(1)	(2)	(3)	(4)	(5)
1.	1983–84	570	13,657.76	23.96
2.	1984–85	570	13,087.20	22.96
3.	1985–86	547	14,237.17	26.03
4.	1986–88	533	25,526.02	47.89
5.	1988–89	492	13,765.19	27.98
6.	1989–90	476	24.388.46	51.24
7.	1990–91	464	20,153.41	43.43
8.	1991–92	449	24,274.02	54.06
9.	1992–93	434	25,381.68	58.48
10.	1993–94	423	27,963.87	66.11

Source : Compiled from the Annual Reports and Unpublished Records of the Co-optex.

Table 14.3 reveals that there is a steady increase in the average sales per retail outlet of Co-optex. The good sales performance of retail outlets has been due to the prompt closure of the inefficient retail outlets.

Pricing Policy of Co-optex

The price is the most important factor among the various elements of marketing mix. It is the only element in the mix that produces revenues, whereas all the other elements such as product, place and promotion represent only the cost. It affects every other aspect of the business namely sales, revenue, profit, demand and perception of quality. Total revenue realised by Co-optex depends on the price per unit and the total units sold. It creates clientele and it fixes and the tone of competition. It is simply an offer to the consumer and a means to know the customer's reaction towards the fabrics marketed by Co-optex.

The important factors that are considered by the Co-optex in fixing the prices are:

a) Cost of procurement,

b) Sales target,

c) Competition,

d) Government Policy,

e) Growth rate,

f) Maintaining the goodwill of Co-optex and

g) Stability in price.

The handloom weavers' co-operatives including Co-optex follow the cost-plus-pricing method to fix the base price for their products.

In handloom co-operative the cost of the production of each unit of handloom fabrics is computed by taking into account the direct material cost and direct labour cost incurred in producing the fabrics. The societies do not take into account overheads, inventory carrying cost and such other indirect costs.

The Co-optex procures the fabrics produced by the primaries. The primaries are allowed to have a profit margin of 10 to 29 per cent over and above their cost of production. Since the same variety of cloth is produced by different societies, it results in different production costs. In order to ensure uniform price for a single variety of fabric produced by different societies, the Directorate of Handlooms has fixed an upper price limit for each variety of fabric. The Co-optex pays either the price administered by the Directorate of Handlooms or the price quoted by the primaries which ever is less.

The Co-optex fixes its selling price by adding 15 to 40 per cent margin to its procurement price. For silk and polyester fabrics, the margin is 35 to 40 per cent, It is 15 to 20 per cent for janatha cloths and 20 to 25 per cent for cotton fabrics. The Co-optex adopts a differential margins to fix the selling price for its products. The selling price of Co-optex has two profit margins. The first profit margin is allowed to producing societies and the second profit margin is added to the sale price by Co-optex. Hence, there is a higher price for the fabrics sold by Co-optex than that in the showrooms of primaries.

The selling price of the Co-optex fabrics is uniform in all the retail outlets within the State of Tamil Nadu. But, it is three per cent more for the sales made outside Tamil Nadu. This has been due to additional freight cost. The Co-optex adopts "place price discrimination policy" towards the consumers in Tamil Nadu and those in other State of India.

Promoting Products

Advertising

Advertising refers to any paid form of non-personal presentation and promotion of ideas, goods or services by an identified paying sponsor.

The Co-optex also make use of the services of private marketing agencies for its advertisement. Co-optex has diversified its advertising techniques to popularise the fabrics of cotton, silk, polyester sarees, dress materials, shirtings and the like.

Co-optex advertises its handloom fabrics through the following media:

1. Television,
2. Radio,
3. Newspapers and Magazines,
4. Slides in Cinema Theatres,
5. Bit Notices,
6. Writings on walls,
7. Advertisement in buses and trains
8. Advertisement Banners,

9. Advertisement hoardings,
10. Neon Sign advertisements and
11. Distribution of stickers.

The advertisement in the press, radio and television in done by Co-optex only during the eve of festival seasons like Deepavali, Pongal, Handloom Week and the like.

Sales Promotion

For promoting the sale of handloom fabrics, important sales promotional efforts undertaken by Co-optex include the following:

1. Sales through Retail Outlets
2. Rebate on Sales
3. Participates in Exhibitions
4. Showrooms
5. Beauty contests and the like.

Retail Outlets

In order to promote the sale of handloom fabrics, co-optex has opened 423 retail outlets within and outside India. The sales depots are suitably furnished with racks and show cases for exhibiting handloom fabrics. Every retail outlets has a minimum of two to three sales persons to attend to the customers visiting the shop. The showrooms are generally kept open for sale both in the mornings and the evenings to suit the conveniences of the customers. They operate between 9.30 a.m. and 2. p.m. and between 4 p.m. and 8 p.m. During the festival seasons like Deepavali and Pongal, they function continuously without a break.

Rebate Scheme

In order to encourage sales, rebate on sales is given to consumers during the festival seasons and on the birthdays of important leaders like Mahatma Gandhiji and Anna. Under the rebate scheme, handloom fabrics are sold at the discounted price. The loss on sale price due to the rebate is claimed by the primaries at a later date from the State Government.

The rebate on handloom sales is allowed for a maximum of 100 days in a year on the eve of the following occasion and festivals:

1. Summer sales
2. Handloom festival

3. Adi festival
4. Raksha Bandan
5. Ganesh Pooja
6. Onam festival
7. Anna and Periya Birthdays
8. Durga Pooja
9. Deepavali
10. Marriage day seasons
11. Pongal
12. Christmas
13. Chief Minister's Birthday
14. Ramzan
15. Clearance Sales Period and
16. Holi.

The rebate helps the handloom co-operatives to sell the fabrics at low prices and turn competitive in the market. It has accelerated the sales volume of the handloom fabrics throughout India and it has helped the handloom co-operatives to clear the accumulated stocks. From October 1997 onwards rebate is given to consumers throughout the year.

Exhibitions and Trade Fairs

Exhibitions and trade fairs are organised by the Development Commissioner for Handlooms and Textiles Government of India to promote the sale of handloom fabrics. Co-optex takes active part by opening stalls in the handloom exhibitions.

Beauty Contests

To induce the youth to purchase Co-optex products, Co-optex has organised handloom contests and fashion shows. One such contest was organised at the World University Centre at Madras on February 28, 1988 and another show at Madras was also conducted in 1995. The prizes were awarded to the winner queens.

Conclusion

Co-optex procures the handloom fabrics produced by the weaver's co-operative societies in Tamil Nadu through its 11 regional procurement centres The major items of fabrics sold by Co-optex include silk fabrics, cotton fabrics, polyester fabrics and janatha fabrics. Co-optex has 423 retails outlets. Co-optex fixes its selling price by adding 15 to 40 per cent margin to its procurement price. Co-optex uses advertisement and sales promotional efforts to increase the sale volume of handloom fabrics. In order to encourage handloom sales, rebate on sales in given to consumers throughout the year from October 1997 onwards. Co-optex has been exporting wide range of handloom fabrics to many countries.

15

A Study on the Buyer Behaviour of the Co-operative Silk Sarees

*Dr. Punithavathy Pandian**

*Mrs. A. I. Auxilia Felcitas***

Silk is associated with glamour and sophistication. Once it was the garment of kings and nobility and regarded as the queen of textiles. Even today it is rather expensive when compared to other fabrics, yet the craze for this has in no way has come down. Specially in Tamil Nadu, no marriage or festival goes without the ladies wearing the glittering gold laced silk sarees.

The country's first primary co-operative society was established at Kancheepuram in 1905. Co-optex was established in Tamil Nadu in 1935, with the objectives of organising and promoting handloom industry in the state on a commercial basis. The silk fabric production has got a prominent place in the co-operative textile units in the heritage of Tamil Nadu. Handloom silk products fetch higher price per unit and higher wages for the weavers. To help the industry and its weavers the Government encouraged co-operative sector and primary weavers co-operative societies were formed. The success of any society depends on the demand for its products. Each consumer is a separate individual with a unique personality and the preference varies from one to another. The buyer behaviour has to be studied in detail to satisfy the needs of the consumers which in turn generates profits to the societies. This chapter analyses the buyer behaviour of the silk products of silk society.

Data: Madurai is one among the handloom centres in Tamil Nadu and many co-operative societies are producing silk sarees. Among them

* Professor of Commerce, Madurai—Kamraj University, Madurai—625 021

**Department of Commerce, Fatima College, Madurai.

Srinivasa Perumal Weavers Co-operative society which is making profit continuously for 20 years has been selected for the study purpose. Structured schedules were administered to 150 buyers of the society's product to study the buyer behaviour.

Tools of Analysis : Chi-square test has been used for testing the various hypotheses formulated in the study.

where,

$$\chi^2 = \Sigma \frac{(O-E)^2}{E}$$

O = observed frequency

E = Expected frequency

Weighted arithmetic mean is also used in the study.

Occasion of Purchase of Silk Sarees

In some families silk sarees the purchased regularly and in some other families they are purchased for marriage or festivals. The occasion of purchase of silk sarees by the respondents in accordance with their monthly income is presented in Table 15.1.

Table 15.1 : Occasion of Purchase of Silk Sarees

Income Rs.	*Occasion*		*Total*
	Marriage/ Festival	*Regular*	
Upto 4000	10	---	10
4000 – 6000	19	2	21
6000 – 8000	48	6	54
8000 – 10000	28	13	41
Above 10000	10	14	24
Total	**115**	**35**	**150**

The Table 15.1 shows that 115 consumers out of the total 150 sample consumers, purchase silk sarees only for marriage or festivals. Only 35 of the sample consumers purchase silk sarees regularly. Though there is a preference for silk among the consumers, the purchase of silk is normally occasional. The purchase is limited by the purchasing power. Yet, there are consumers who purchase silk sarees regularly. This may be due to various reasons like neighbours' pressure, status maintenance, less expenditure on food, custom, and innate desire for silk. To prove statistically that income has influence on the regularity of purchase of silk sarees, the following hypotheses were formulated. For calculation of χ^2 the income group was divided into two groups i.e. above Rs. 6000 and below Rs. 6000.

Ho : Income has no influence on the regularity of purchase of silk sarees.

H_A : Income has influence on the regularity of purchase of silk sarees.

Chi Square Test is used to test the null hypothesis. The calculated value of Chi-square is : $\chi^2 = 21.237$

It is more than the table value 3.84 (v = 1) at 5 per cent level of signature. Hence the null hypothesis is rejected. This shows that income has a profound influence on the regularity of purchase. Even though the lower income group desires silk, it is beyond their means to purchase it regularly. But it is different in the case of the higher income group, where the basic needs are met and they are also to buy silk sarees at higher prices.

Income and Price Range of the Saree Purchased

Income is an important factor determining the purchasing power. The range of the price of the saree purchased depends on the affordability of the person purchasing and this affordability in turn depends on the income of the family. Table 15.2 shows the monthly income of the family of the respondents and the range of the price of the silk saree purchased by them.

The Table 15.2 shows that majority of the respondents belongs to the income group of above Rs. 8000/- p.m. In that category silk

Tabld 15.2 : Income and Price Range of the Saree Purchased

Monthly Income (Rs.)	*Price of the Silk Saree (Rs.)*			*Total*
	2000–3500	*3500–5000*	*Above 5000*	
Upto 6000	8	11	12	31
6000 – 8000	11	20	23	54
Above 8000	18	18	29	65
Total	37	49	64	150

Source : Survey Data.

sarees costing above Rs. 5000/- are purchased by 45 per cent of the respondents and sarees costing Rs. 2000-3500 and Rs. 3500-5000 are purchased by equal proportion of the respondent (27.5% each). Out of the respondents belonging to the income group of Rs. 6000-8000, 43 per cent purchased sarees costing above Rs. 5000/- and among the respondents belonging to the income group of upto Rs. 6,000 39 per cent purchased sarees worth above Rs. 5000/-. This shows that with the rise in income costly sarees are purchased.

Reasons for Purchasing Silk Sarees

Among the various reasons influencing the purchase of silk sarees five important reasons were chosen and the sample consumers ranked the reasons according to their preferences. The reason influenced the purchase of silk and the ranks given by the sample consumers are given in Table 15.3.

Table 15.3 : Reasons for Purchasing Silk Sarees

Sl. No.	*Reasons*	*Ranks* I	II	III	IV	V	*Total*
1.	Innate Desire	36	54	30	22	8	150
2.	Attractive	17	36	29	42	26	150
3.	Status Symbol	30	24	48	35	13	150
4.	Custom	48	19	17	32	34	150
5.	Compulsion by family members	19	17	26	19	69	150
	Total	150	150	150	150	150	

Source : Survey Data.

Among the factors influencing the first two viz., Inate Desire and Attraction are internal factors. These are the factors which arise from within oneself, individualistic and personal in nature. The other factors viz, status symbol, custom and conpulsion by family members are external factors. The influence of the society or family to which the consumers belong is more one these factors than the personal or individual influence.

In order to find out the most important reason which influenced the purchase of silk sarees the weighted average method is used. The scores and the weighted arithmetic mean of the different reasons are shown in Table 15.4.

Table 15.4 : Weighted Arithmetic Mean

Reasons	*Scores*	*W.A.M.*
Innate Desire	538	35.87
Attractive	426	28.4
Status Symbol	473	31.5
Custom	465	31.0
Compulsion by family members	348	23.2

Source : Suvey Data.

The Table 15.4 indicates that, it is inate desire, the internal factor which influence the buyers, the most to purchase silk sarees. The next important reason is the status symbol, the external factor. The other external factor viz., custom also exert an equal pressure on the consumers in purchasing silk sarees like status symbol.

Pattern Preferred

Every women has an inborn desire of looking unique, and each female does not prefer to wear the same type of clothing worn by another. This uniqueness is expressed in the colour of the saree, pattern of the saree and many other minute things. Pattern of the saree is one which contributes more to the uniqueness. The pattern of the saree preferred in accordance with the age of the sample consumers is given in Table 15.5.

Table 15.5 : Pattern of the Saree Preferred

Age in Years	*Pattern of the Saree*		*Total*
	Single Bordered	*Double Bordered*	
Upto 30	9	15	24
30 – 40	50	22	72
Above 40	46	8	54
Total	105	45	150

Source : Survey Data

The Table 15.5 show that the pattern of the saree preferred varies according to the age group of the consumers. For example, around 85 per cent of the respondents in the age group of 40 years, 69 per cent of the respondents in the age group of 30-40 years preferred single bordered sarees. This shows that age has a strong influence in choosing a particular pattern of the saree. In order to prove this statically, the following hypotheses were formulated.

H_o : Age has no influence on the pattern preference.

H_A : Age has an influence on the pattern preference.

Chi-square Test is used to the hypothesis. The calculated value of the Chi-square. $\chi^2 = 18.01$. It is more than the table value 5.99 (υ–2) at 5 per cent level of the significance. Hence, the null hypothesis is rejected and it could be concluded that age has its influence in the pattern preference.

Appearance of the Silk Saree

The sample consumers are classified according to their literacy level and their taste as far as the appearance of the silk saree is divided into two viz., Simple and Grand.

In this study a simple saree means a saree with small zari border and a few designs/putta. A grand saree is one with big thick zari borders and designs/putta. Normally, the price of the simple saree is less than the price of the grand saree as the price varies according to the quantity of zari used in the saree. But there are cases, where a saree appears to be simple costs more than the other and this may be due to the design and pattern of the particular saree. The educational qualification of the respondents and their taste of appearance of the saree are shown in Table 15.6.

Table 15.6 : Literacy Level and Appearance of the Silk Saree

Educational Qualification	*Appearance of the Saree*		*Total*
	Simple	*Grand*	
Higher Secondary/PUC	33	37	70
Graduates	16	20	36
Post-Graduates and Professionals	37	7	44
Total	**86**	**64**	**150**

Source : Survey Data

The Table 15.6 shows that the taste of the respondents vary considerably according to their literacy level. For instance, around 84 per cent of the consumers who are post graduates or professionally qualified preferred their sarees to appear simple, and 53 per cent of the respondents who are educated upto Higher Secondary or below preferred their sarees to appear grand. To establish this statistically the following hypotheses were formulated.

H_O: Literacy level is not determining the appearance of the silk saree purchased.

H_A: Literacy level is determining the appearance of the silk saree purchased.

The calculated value is $\chi^2 = 18.28$. It is more than the table value 5.99 ($\nu = 2$) at 5 per cent of significance. Hence, the null hypothesis is rejected and it could be concluded that literacy level has its influence on the appearance of the silk saree purchased.

Marital Status and Appearance of the Saree

To test whether marital status has any role to play in the appearance of the saree purchased the respondents are classified according to their marital status and their taste for the appearance of the saree (Table 15.7).

Table 15.7 : Marital Status and Appearance of Silk Saree

Marital Status	*Appearance of the Saree*		*Total*
	Simple	*Grand*	
Married	75	57	132
Unmarried	11	7	18
Total	**86**	**64**	**150**

Source : Survey Data

To establish statistically the effect the marital status on the appearance of the silk saree purchased, the following hypotheses are formulated :

H_o: Marital Status has no influence on the appearance of the silk saree purchased.

H_A: Marital Status has its influence on the appearance of the silk saree purchased.

Chi-square test is used the validity of the hypotheses formulated. The calculated value of Chi-square, $\chi^2 = 0.1064$. It is less than the table value 3.84 (ν–1) at 5 per cent level of significance. Hence, the null hypotheses is accepted and it could be concluded that marital status has no influence on the appearance of the silk saree purchased.

Colour Combinations Preferred

Colours make any fabric more attractive and add beauty to the garment. As silk sarees are preserved by consumers as jewels the colour of the saree plays a very important role. Moreover, beliefs and values are attached to colours throughout the world. The various colour combinations preferred by the sample consumers are shown in Table 15.8.

Table 15.8 : Colour Combinations Preferred

Sl. No.	*Colour Combinations*	*No. of Respondents*	*Percentage*
1.	Blue with other colours	43	28.67
2.	Green with other colours	39	26.00
3.	Red with other colours	28	18.67
4.	Pink with other colours	17	11.33
5.	yellow with other colours	12	8.00
6.	Other combinations	11	7.33
	Total	150	100.00

Source : Suvey Data.

The Table 15.8 shows that majority of the respondents prefer dark colour. The main reason for this is that the zari work is very bright on the dark colours. Blue with other colours, is preferred by majority of the consumers (28.67%) as blue goes well with all colours and the zari work also is very conspicuous. Green colour is associated with flourishment and fertility and it is preferred by 26 per cent of the respondents. Like wise, values and beliefs are attached to each and every colour. The society staff reported that normally consumers from Kerala prefer white with other combinations.

Reasons for Purchasing from the Society

About 58 per cent of the sample consumers have made repeated purchases from the society. These consumers alongwith the consumers who have made their purchase from the society for the first time have ranked the factors influenced them to make the purchase from the society. The information are presented in Table 15.9.

Tabld 15.9 : Reasons for Purchasing Silk Sarees from the Societies

Sl. No.	Reasons	Ranks I	II	III	Total
1.	Quality	72	42	36	150
2.	Discount	49	63	38	150
3.	Courteous and Obliging Staff	29	45	76	150
	Total	150	150	150	

In order to find out the most important factor influencing the buyer towards the society the weighted average method is used. The scores and the weighted arithmetic means of the different reasons are shown in Table 15.10.

Table 15.10 : Weighted Arithmetic Mean

Sl. No.	Reasons	Scores	W.A.M.
1.	Quality	336	56.00
2.	Discount	311	51.83
3.	Courteous and Obliging Staff	253	42.17

Source : Suvey Data.

Table 15.10 indicates that quality is the most important factor influencing the consumers to purchase from the society, followed by discount and courteous staff respectively.

Decision Maker in the Purchase of the Silk Saree

At the time of purchasing sarees a number of the sarees are displayed to the consumers and out of the displayed saree the selection is made. The selection decision may be made by the individual, friends or the family members. Table 15.11 presents the information regarding the selection decision.

The Table 15.11 indicates that in the case of around 59 per cent of the respondents, the selection decision is taken jointly by the individual who wears the saree and the family members. In the case of 24.67 per cent of the sample consumers the selection decision is made by the individual who wears and in the case of 16 per cent of

Table 15.11 : Silk Sarees Selection Decision

Sl. No.	*Decision Maker*	*No. of Respondents*	*Percentage*
1.	Individual who wears the Saree	37	24.67
2.	Individual and the family members	89	59.33
3.	Male members of the family	24	16.00
	Total	150	100.00

Source : Suvey Data.

the respondents the decision is taken by the male members of the family. This indicates that only in very few families the selection decision is made by the male members of the family.

Time Consumed in Choosing and Purchasing Silk Sarees

The general remark is that the women are not time conscious in the sarees selection. It is even more for silk sarees. The age of the respondents and the time spent by them in choosing and purchasing a silk saree are presented in Table 15.12.

Table 15.12 : Age and Time Consumed in Purchasing Silk Saree

Age in Years	*Time Consumed*		*Total*
	Less than ½ an hr.	*More than ½ an hr.*	
Upto 30	12	12	24
30 – 40	39	33	72
Above 40	29	25	54
Total	**80**	**70**	**150**

Source : Survey Data

The Table 15.12 indicates that 26 per cent of the respondents spend less than half an hour and they belong to the age group of 30-40 years and 16.67 per cent of the respondents spend more than one hour and they are in the age group of above 40 years. So, in order to test whether age has any role in play on the time consumed in purchasing silk sarees the following hypotheses are formulated :

H_o: Age is not influencing the time consumed in purchasing silk saree.

H_A: Age is influencing the time consumed in purchasing silk sarees.

Chiq-square is used to test the hypothesis. The calculated value of Chi-square $\chi^2 = 0.1188$. It is less than the table value 3.84 $(\nu - 1)$ at 5 per cent level of significance. Hence, the hypothesis is accepted and it could be concluded that age has no influence on the time consumed in purchasing silk sarees.

Conclusion

The desire for silk is inherent in every woman irrespective of the age, income, education and the locality of living. Normally, silk sarees are purchased for marriage or festival occasions. Age plays an important role in the pattern of the sarees purchased and nature of the saree purchased is influenced by the literacy level. It is the quality which attracts the consumers to the society for pure silk saree purchase.